THE MEMBER OF
THE WEDDING

Wit   elicacy of perception and memory,
hum   : and pathos, Carson McCullers
spre   before us the three phases of a
w   nd crisis in the life of a motherless
t   year-old girl. Within the span of a few
         the irresistible, hoydenish Frankie
         nately plays out her fantasies at her
         brother's wedding. Through a perilous
s.   it we look right into the mind of a
         torn between the yearning to belong
         e urge to run away.

FOR ELIZABETH AMES

The Member Of The Wedding

by

Carson McCullers

Dales Large Print Books
Long Preston, North Yorkshire,
BD23 4ND, England.

British Library Cataloguing in Publication Data.

McCullers, Carson
    The member of the wedding.

    A catalogue record of this book is
    available from the British Library

    ISBN   978-1-84262-520-0 pbk

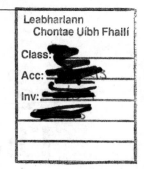
First published in Great Britain in 1947 by The Cresset Press

Cover illustration © Gordon Crabb by arrangement with
Alison Eldred

The moral right of the author has been asserted

Published in Large Print 2007 by arrangement with
Pollinger Limited

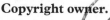

Dales Large Print is an imprint of Library Magna Books Ltd.

Printed and bound in Great Britain by
T.J. (International) Ltd., Cornwall, PL28 8RW

PART I

It happened that green and crazy summer when Frankie was twelve years old. This was the summer when for a long time she had not been a member. She belonged to no club and was a member of nothing in the world. Frankie had become an unjoined person who hung around in doorways, and she was afraid. In June the trees were bright dizzy green, but later the leaves darkened, and the town turned black and shrunken under the glare of the sun. At first Frankie walked around doing one thing and another. The sidewalks of the town were grey in the early morning and at night, but the noon sun put a glaze on them, so that the cement burned and glittered like glass. The sidewalks finally became too hot for Frankie's feet, and also she got herself in trouble. She was in so much secret trouble that she thought it was better to stay at home – and at home there was only Berenice Sadie Brown and John Henry West. The three of them sat at the kitchen table, saying the same things over and over, so that by August the words began to rhyme with each other and sound strange. The world seemed to die each afternoon and nothing moved any longer. At last the summer was like a green sick dream, or like a silent crazy jungle under glass. And then, on the last Friday of August, all this was changed: it was so sudden that Frankie puzzled the whole blank afternoon, and still she did not understand.

'It is so very queer,' she said. 'The way it all just happened.'

'Happened? Happened?' said Berenice. John Henry listened and watched them quietly.

'I have never been so puzzled.'

'But puzzled about what?'

'The whole thing,' Frankie said.

And Berenice remarked: 'I believe the sun has fried your brains.'

'Me too,' John Henry whispered.

Frankie herself almost admitted maybe so. It was four o'clock in the afternoon and the kitchen was square and grey and quiet. Frankie sat at the table with her eyes half closed, and she thought about a wedding. She saw a silent church, a strange snow slanting down against the coloured windows. The groom in this wedding was her brother, and there was a brightness where his face should be. The bride was there in a long white train, and the bride also was faceless. There was something about this wedding that gave Frankie a feeling she could not name.

'Look here at me,' said Berenice. 'You jealous?'

'Jealous?'

'Jealous because your brother going to be married?'

'No,' said Frankie. 'I just never saw any two people like them. When they walked in the house today it was so queer.'

'You jealous,' said Berenice. 'Go and behold yourself in the mirror. I can see from the colour in your eye.'

There was a watery kitchen mirror hanging above the sink. Frankie looked, but her eyes were grey as they always were. This summer she was grown so tall that she was almost a big freak, and her shoulders were narrow, her legs too long. She wore a pair of blue track shorts, a B.V.D. undervest, and she was barefooted. Her hair had been cut like a boy's, but it had not been cut for a long time and was now not even parted. The reflection in the glass was warped and crooked, but Frankie knew well what she looked like; she drew up her left shoulder and turned her head aside.

'Oh,' she said. 'They were the two prettiest people I ever saw. I just can't understand how it happened.'

'But what, Foolish?' said Berenice. 'Your brother come home with the girl he means to marry and took dinner today with you and your Daddy. They intend to marry at her home in Winter Hill this coming Sunday. You and your Daddy are going to the wedding. And that is the A and the Z of the matter. So whatever ails you?'

'I don't know,' said Frankie. 'I bet they have a good time every minute of the day.'

'Less us have a good time,' John Henry said.

'Us have a good time?' Frankie asked. 'Us?'

The three of them sat at the table again and Berenice dealt the cards for three-handed bridge. Berenice had been the cook since Frankie could remember. She was very black and broad-shouldered and short. She always said that she was thirty-five years old, but she had been saying that at least three years. Her hair was parted, plaited, and greased close to the skull, and she had a flat and quiet face. There was only one thing wrong about Berenice – her left eye was bright blue glass.

It stared out fixed and wild from her quiet, coloured face, and why she had wanted a blue eye nobody human would ever know. Her right eye was dark and sad. Berenice dealt slowly, licking her thumb when the sweaty cards stuck together. John Henry watched each card as it was being dealt. His chest was white and wet and naked, and he wore around his neck a tiny lead donkey tied by a string. He was blood kin to Frankie, first cousin, and all summer he would eat dinner and spend the day with her, or eat supper and spend the night; and she could not make him go home. He was small to be six years old, but he had the largest knees that Frankie had ever seen, and on one of them there was always a scab or a bandage where he had fallen down and skinned himself. John Henry had a little screwed white face and he wore tiny gold-rimmed glasses. He watched all of the cards very carefully, because he was in debt; he owed Berenice more than five million dollars.

'I bid one heart,' said Berenice.

'A spade,' said Frankie.

'I want to bid spades,' said John Henry. 'That's what I was going to bid.'

'Well, that's your tough luck. I bid them first.'

'Oh, you fool jackass!' he said. 'It's not fair!'

'Hush quarrelling,' said Berenice. 'To tell the truth, I don't think either one of you got such a grand hand to fight over the bid about. I bid two hearts.'

'I don't give a durn about it,' Frankie said. 'It is immaterial with me.'

As a matter of fact this was so: she played bridge that afternoon like John Henry, just putting down any card that suddenly occurred to her. They sat together in the kitchen, and the kitchen was a sad and ugly room. John Henry had covered the walls with queer, child drawings, as far up as his arm would reach. This gave the kitchen a crazy look, like that of a room in the crazy-house. And now the old kitchen made Frankie sick. The name for what had happened to her Frankie did not know, but she could feel her squeezed heart beating against the table edge.

'The world is certainly a small place,' she said.

'What makes you say that?'

'I mean sudden,' said Frankie. 'The world is certainy a sudden place.'

'Well, I don't know,' said Berenice. 'Sometimes sudden and sometimes slow.'

Frankie's eyes were half closed, and to her

own ears her voice sounded ragged, far away: 'To me it is sudden.'

For only yesterday Frankie had never thought seriously about a wedding. She knew that her only brother, Jarvis, was to be married. He had become engaged to a girl in Winter Hill just before he went to Alaska. Jarvis was a corporal in the army and he had spent almost two years in Alaska. Frankie had not seen her brother for a long, long time, and his face had become masked and changing, like a face seen under water. But Alaska! Frankie had dreamed of it constantly, and especially this summer it was very real. She saw the snow and frozen sea and ice glaciers. Eskimo igloos and polar bears and the beautiful Northern Lights. When Jarvis had first gone to Alaska, she had sent him a box of home-made fudge, packing it carefully and wrapping each piece separately in waxed paper. It had thrilled her to think that her fudge would be eaten in Alaska, and she had a vision of her brother passing it around to furry Eskimos. Three months later, a thank-you letter had come from Jarvis with a five-dollar bill enclosed. For a while she mailed candy almost every week, sometimes divinity instead of fudge, but Jarvis did not send her another bill, except at Christmas time.

Sometimes his short letters to her father disturbed her a little. For instance, this summer he mentioned once that he had been in swimming and that the mosquitoes were something fierce. This letter jarred upon her dream, but after a few days of bewilderment, she returned to her frozen seas and snow. When Jarvis had come back from Alaska, he had gone straight to Winter Hill. The bride was named Janice Evans and the plans for the wedding were like this: her brother had wired that he and the bride were coming this Friday to spend the day, then on the following Sunday there was to be the wedding at Winter Hill. Frankie and her father were going to the wedding, travelling nearly a hundred miles to Winter Hill, and Frankie had already packed a suitcase. She looked forward to the time her brother and the bride should come, but she did not picture them to herself, and did not think about the wedding. So on the day before the visit she only commented to Berenice:

'I think it's a curious coincidence that Jarvis would get to go to Alaska and that the very bride he picked to marry would come from a place called Winter Hill. Winter Hill,' she repeated slowly, her eyes closed, and the name blended with dreams of Alaska and cold snow. 'I wish tomorrow was Sunday instead of Friday. I wish I had already left town.'

'Sunday will come,' said Berenice.

'I doubt it,' said Frankie. 'I've been ready to leave this town so long. I wish I didn't have to come back here after the wedding. I wish I was going somewhere for good. I wish I had a hundred dollars and could just light out and never see this town again.'

'It seems to me you wish for a lot of things,' said Berenice.

'I wish I was somebody else except me.'

So the afternoon before it happened was like the other August afternoons. Frankie had hung around the kitchen, then towards dark she had gone out into the yard. The scuppernong arbour behind the house was purple and dark in the twilight. She walked slowly. John Henry West was sitting beneath the August arbour in a wicker chair, his legs crossed and his hands in his pockets.

'What are you doing?' she asked.

'I'm thinking.'

'About what?'

He did not answer.

Frankie was too tall this summer to walk beneath the arbour as she had always done before. Other twelve-year-old people could

13

still walk around inside, give shows, and have a good time. Even small grown ladies could walk underneath the arbour. And already Frankie was too big; this year she had to hang around and pick from the edges like the grown people. She stared into the tangle of dark vines, and there was the smell of crushed scuppernongs and dust. Standing beside the arbour with dark coming on, Frankie was afraid. She did not know what caused this fear, but she was afraid.

'I tell you what,' she said. 'Suppose you eat supper and spend the night with me.'

John Henry took his dollar watch from his pocket and looked at it as though the time would decide whether or not he would come, but it was too dark under the arbour for him to read the numbers.

'Go on home and tell Aunt Pet. I'll meet you in the kitchen.'

'All right.'

She was afraid. The evening sky was pale and empty and the light from the kitchen window made a yellow square reflection in the darkening yard. She remembered that when she was a little girl she believed that three ghosts were living in the coalhouse, and one of the ghosts wore a silver ring.

She ran up the back steps and said: 'I just

now invited John Henry to eat supper and spend the night with me.'

Berenice was kneading a lump of biscuit dough, and she dropped it on the flour-dusted table. 'I thought you were sick and tired of him.'

'I am sick and tired of him,' said Frankie. 'But it seemed to me he looked scared.'

'Scared of what?'

Frankie shook her head. 'Maybe I mean lonesome,' she said finally.

'Well, I'll save him a scrap of dough.'

After the darkening yard the kitchen was hot and bright and queer. The walls of the kitchen bothered Frankie – the queer drawings of Christmas trees, aeroplanes, freak soldiers, flowers. John Henry had started the first pictures one long afternoon in June, and having already ruined the wall, he went on and drew whenever he wished. Sometimes Frankie had drawn also. At first her father had been furious about the walls, but later he said for them to draw all the pictures out of their systems, and he would have the kitchen painted in the fall. But as the summer lasted, and would not end, the walls had begun to bother Frankie. That evening the kitchen looked strange to her, and she was afraid.

She stood in the doorway and said: 'I just

thought I might as well invite him.'

So at dark John Henry came to the back door with a little week-end bag. He was dressed in his white recital suit and had put on shoes and socks. There was a dagger buckled to his belt. John Henry had seen snow. Although he was only six years old, he had gone to Birmingham last winter, and there he had seen snow. Frankie had never seen snow.

'I'll take the week-end bag,' said Frankie. 'You can start right in making a biscuit man.'

'O.K.'

John Henry did not play with the dough; he worked on the biscuit man as though it were a very serious business. Now and then he stopped off, settled his glasses with his little hand, and studied what he had done. He was like a tiny watchmaker, and he drew up a chair and knelt on it so that he could get directly over the work. When Berenice gave him some raisins, he did not stick them all around as any other human child would do; he used only two for the eyes: but immediately he realized they were too large – so he divided one raisin carefully and put in eyes, two specks for the nose, and a little grinning raisin mouth. When he had finished, he wiped his hands on the seat of his shorts, and there was a little biscuit man with separate fingers, a hat on, and even walking stick. John Henry had worked so hard that the dough was now grey and wet. But it was a perfect little biscuit man, and, as a matter of fact, it reminded Frankie of John Henry himself.

'I better entertain you now,' she said.

They ate supper at the kitchen table with Berenice, since her father had telephoned that he was working late at his jewellery store. When Berenice brought the biscuit man from the oven, they saw that it looked exactly like any biscuit man ever made by a child – it had swelled so that all the work of John Henry had been cooked out, the fingers were run together, and the walking stick resembled a sort of tail. But John Henry just looked at it through his glasses, wiped it with his napkin, and buttered the left foot.

It was a dark, hot August night. The radio in the dining-room was playing a mixture of many stations: a war voice crossed with the gabble of an advertiser, and underneath there was the sleazy music of a sweet band. The radio had stayed on all the summer long, so finally it was a sound that as a rule they did not notice. Sometimes, when the noise became so loud, that they could not hear their own ears, Frankie would turn it down a little. Otherwise, music and voices came and went and crossed and twisted with each other, and by August they did not listen any more.

'What do you want to do?' asked Frankie. 'Would you like for me to read to you out of Hans Brinker or would you rather do something else?'

'I rather do something else,' he said.

'What?'

'Less play out.'

'I don't want to,' Frankie said.

'There's a big crowd going to play out tonight.'

'You got ears,' Frankie said. 'You heard me.'

John Henry stood with his big knees locked, then finally he said: 'I think I better go home.'

'Why, you haven't spent the night! You can't eat supper and just go on off like that.'

'I know it,' he said quietly. Along with the radio they could hear the voices of the children playing in the night. 'But less go out, Frankie. They sound like they having a mighty good time.'

'No they're not,' she said. 'Just a lot of ugly silly children. Running and hollering and running and hollering. Nothing to it. We'll go upstairs and unpack your weekend bag.'

Frankie's room was an elevated sleeping porch which had been built on to the house, with a stairway leading up from the kitchen. The room was furnished with an iron bed, a bureau, and a desk. Also Frankie had a motor which could be turned on and off; the motor could sharpen knives, and, if they were long enough, it could be used for filing down your finger-nails. Against the wall was the suitcase packed and ready for the trip to Winter Hill. On the desk there was a very old typewriter, and Frankie sat down before it, trying to think of any letters she could write: but there was nobody for her to write to, as every possible letter had already been answered, and answered even several times. So she covered the typewriter with a rain-coat and pushed it aside.

'Honestly,' John Henry said, 'don't you think I better go home?'

'No,' she answered, without looking around at him. 'You sit there in the corner and play with the motor.'

Before Frankie there were now two objects – a lavender seashell and a glass globe with snow inside that could be shaken into a snowstorm. When she held the seashell to her ear, she could hear the warm wash of the Gulf of Mexico, and think of a green palm island far away. And she could hold the snow globe to her narrowed eyes and watch the whirling white flakes fall until they blinded her. She dreamed of Alaska. She walked up a cold white hill and looked on a snowy wasteland far below. She watched the sun make colours in the ice, and heard dream voices, saw dream things. And everywhere there was the cold white gentle snow.

'Look,' John Henry said, and he was staring out of the window. 'I think those big girls are having a party in their clubhouse.'

'Hush!' Frankie screamed suddenly. 'Don't mention those crooks to me.'

There was in the neighbourhood a clubhouse, and Frankie was not a member. The members of the club were girls who were thirteen and fourteen and even fifteen years old. They had parties with boys on Saturday night. Frankie knew all of the club members, and until this summer she had been like a younger member of their crowd, but now they had this club and she was not a member. They had said she was too young and mean. On Saturday night she could hear the terrible music and see from far away their light. Sometimes she went around to the alley behind the clubhouse and stood near a honeysuckle fence. She stood in the alley and watched and listened. They were very long, those parties.

'Maybe they will change their mind and invite you,' John Henry said.

'The son-of-a-bitches.'

Frankie sniffled and wiped her nose in the crook of her arm. She sat down on the edge of the bed, her shoulders slumped and her elbows resting on her knees. 'I think they have been spreading it all over town that I smell bad,' she said. 'When I had those boils and that black bitter smelling ointment, old Helen Fletcher asked what was that funny smell I had. Oh, I could shoot every one of them with a pistol.'

She heard John Henry walking up to the bed, and then she felt his hand patting her neck with tiny little pats. 'I don't think you smell so bad,' he said. 'You smell sweet.'

'The son-of-a-bitches,' she said again. 'And there was something else. They were talking nasty lies about married people. When I think of Aunt Pet and Uncle Ustace. And my own father! The nasty lies! I don't know what kind of fool they take me for.'

'I can smell you the minute you walk in the house without even looking to see if it is you. Like a hundred flowers.'

'I don't care,' she said. 'I just don't care.'

'Like a thousand flowers,' said John Henry, and still he was patting his sticky hand on the back of her bent neck.

Frankie sat up, licked the tears from around her mouth, and wiped off her face with her shirt tail. She sat still, her nose widened, smelling herself. Then she went to her suitcase and took out a bottle of Sweet Serenade. She rubbed some on the top of her head and poured some more down inside the neck of her shirt.

'Want some on you?'

John Henry was squatting beside the open suitcase and he gave a little shiver when she poured the perfume over him. He wanted to meddle in her travelling suitcase and look carefully at everything she owned. But Frankie only wanted him to get a general impression, and not count and know just what she had and what she did not have. So she strapped the suitcase and pushed it back against the wall.

'Boy!' she said. 'I bet I use more perfume than anybody in this town.'

The house was quiet except for the low rumble of the radio in the dining-room downstairs. Long ago her father had come home and Berenice had closed the back door and gone away. There was no longer the sound of children's voices in the summer night.

'I guess we ought to have a good time,' said Frankie.

But there was nothing to do. John Henry stood, his knees locked and his hands clasped behind his back, in the middle of the room. There were moths at the window – pale green moths and yellow moths that fluttered and spread their wings against the screen.

'Those beautiful butterflies,' he said. 'They are trying to get in.'

Frankie watched the soft moths tremble and press against the window screen. The moths came every evening when the lamp on her desk was lighted. They came from out of the August night and fluttered and clung against the screen.

'To me it is the irony of fate,' she said. 'The way they come here. Those moths could fly anywhere. Yet they keep hanging around the windows of this house.'

John Henry touched the gold rim of his glasses to settle them on his nose and Frankie studied his flat little freckled face.

'Take off those glasses,' she said suddenly.

John Henry took them off and blew on them. She looked through the glasses and the room was loose and crooked. Then she pushed back her chair and stared at John Henry. There were two damp white circles around his eyes.

'I bet you don't need those glasses,' she said. She put her hand down on the typewriter. 'What is this?'

'The typewriter,' he said.

Frankie picked up the shell. 'And this?'

'The shell from the Bay.'

'What is that little thing crawling there on the floor?'

'Where?' he asked, looking around him.

'That little thing crawling along near your feet.'

'Oh,' he said. He squatted down. 'Why, it's an ant. I wonder how it got up here.'

Frankie tilted back in her chair and crossed her bare feet on her desk. 'If I were you I'd just throw those glasses away,' she said. 'You can see good as anybody.'

John Henry did not answer.

'They don't look becoming.'

She handed the folded glasses to John Henry and he wiped them with his pink flannel glasses rag. He put them back on and did not answer.

'O.K.' she said. 'Suit yourself. I was only telling you for your own good.'

They went to bed. They undressed with

their backs turned to each other and then Frankie switched off the motor and the light. John Henry knelt down to say his prayers and he prayed for a long time, not saying the words aloud. Then he lay down beside her.

'Good night,' she said.

'Good night.'

Frankie stared up into the dark. 'You know it is still hard for me to realize that the world turns around at the rate of about a thousand miles an hour.'

'I know it,' he said.

'And to understand why it is that when you jump up in the air you don't come down in Fairview or Selma or somewhere fifty miles away.'

John Henry turned over and made a sleepy sound.

'Or Winter Hill,' she said. 'I wish I was starting for Winter Hill right now.'

Already John Henry was asleep. She heard him breathe in the darkness, and now she had what she had wanted so many nights that summer; there was somebody sleeping in the bed with her. She lay in the dark and listened to him breathe, then after a while she raised herself on her elbow. He lay freckled and small in the moonlight, his chest white and naked, and one foot hanging from the edge of the bed. Carefully she put her hand on his stomach and moved closer; it felt as though a little clock was ticking inside him and he smelled of sweat and Sweet Serenade. He smelled like a sour little rose. Frankie leaned down and licked him behind the ear. Then she breathed deeply, settled herself with her chin on his sharp damp shoulder, and closed her eyes: for now, with somebody sleeping in the dark with her, she was not so much afraid.

The sun woke them early the next morning, the white August sun. Frankie could not make John Henry go home. He saw the ham Berenice was cooking, and that the special company dinner was going to be good. Frankie's father read the paper in the living-room, then went downtown to wind the watches at his jewellery store.

'If that brother of mine don't bring me a present from Alaska, I will be seriously mad,' said Frankie.

'Me too,' agreed John Henry.

And what were they doing that August morning when her brother and the bride came home? They were sitting in the arbour shade and talking about Christmas. The glare was hard and bright, the sun-drunk bluejays screamed and murdered among themselves. They talked, and their voices tired down into a little tune and they said the same things over and over. They just drowsed in the dark shade of the arbour, and Frankie was a person who had never thought about a wedding. That was the way they were that August morning when her brother and the bride walked in the house.

'Oh, Jesus!' Frankie said. The cards on the table were greasy and the late sun slanted across the yard. 'The world is certainy a sudden place.'

'Well, stop commenting about it,' said Berenice. 'You don't have your mind on the game.'

Frankie, however, had some of her mind on the game. She played the queen of spades, which were trumps, and John Henry threw off a little two of diamonds. She looked at him. He was staring at the back of her hand as though what he wanted and needed was angled eyesight that could cut around corners and read people's cards.

'You got a spade,' said Frankie.

John Henry put his donkey necklace in his mouth and looked away.

'Cheater,' she said.

'Go on and play your spade,' said Berenice. Then he argued: 'It was hid behind the other card.'

'Cheater.'

But still he would not play. He sat there sad and holding up the game.

'Make haste,' said Berenice.

'I can't,' he said finally. 'It's a jack. The only spade I got is a jack. I don't want to play my jack down under Frankie's queen. I'm not going to do it either.'

Frankie threw her cards down on the table. 'See!' she said to Berenice. 'He don't even follow the first beginning laws! He is a child! It is hopeless! Hopeless! Hopeless!'

'Maybe so,' said Berenice.

'Oh,' Frankie said, 'I am sick unto death.'

She sat with her bare feet on the rungs of the chair, her eyes closed, and her chest against the table edge. The red greasy cards were messed together on the table, and the sight of them made Frankie sick. They had played cards after dinner every single afternoon; if you would eat those old cards, they would taste like a combination of all the dinners of that August, together with a sweaty-handed nasty taste. Frankie swept the cards from the table. The wedding was bright and beautiful as snow and the heart in her was mashed. She got up from the table.

'It is a known truth that grey-eyed people

are jealous.'

'I told you I wasn't jealous,' Frankie said, and she was walking fast around the room. 'I couldn't be jealous of one of them without being jealous of them both. I sociate the two of them together.'

'Well, I were jealous when my foster-brother married,' said Berenice. 'I admit that when John married Clorina I sent a warning I would tear the ears off her head. But you see I didn't. Clorina got ears like anybody else. And now I love her.'

'JA,' said Frankie. 'Janice and Jarvis. Isn't that the strangest thing?'

'What?'

'JA,' she said. 'Both their names begin with JA.'

'And? What about it?'

Frankie walked round and round the kitchen table. 'If only my name was Jane,' she said. 'Jane or Jasmine.'

'I don't follow your frame of mind,' said Berenice.

'Jarvis and Janice and Jasmine. See?'

'No,' said Berenice. 'By the way, I heard this morning on the radio that the French people are chasing the Germans out of Paris.'

'Paris,' Frankie repeated in a hollow tone. 'I wonder if it is against the law to change your name. Or to add to it.'

'Naturally. It is against the law.'

'Well, I don't care,' she said. 'F. Jasmine Addams.'

On the staircase leading to her room there was a doll, and John Henry brought it to the table and sat rocking it in his arms. 'You serious when you gave me this,' he said. He pulled up the doll's dress and fingered the real panties and body-waist. 'I will name her Belle.'

Frankie stared at the doll for a minute. 'I don't know what went on in Jarvis's mind when he brought me that doll. Imagine bringing me a doll! And Janice tried to explain that she had pictured me as a little girl. I had counted on Jarvis bringing me something from Alaska.'

'Your face when you unwrapped the package was a study,' said Berenice.

It was a large doll with red hair and china eyes that opened and closed, and yellow eyelashes. John Henry held her in a lying-down position, so that the eyes were shut, and he was now trying to open them by pulling up the eyelashes.

'Don't do that! It makes me nervous. In fact, take that doll somewhere out of my sight.'

John Henry took it to the back porch where he could pick it up when he went home.

'Her name is Lily Belle,' he said.

The clock ticked very slowly on the shelf above the stove, and it was only quarter to six. The glare outside the window was still hard and yellow and bright. In the back yard the shade beneath the arbour was black and solid. Nothing moved. From somewhere far away came the sound of whistling, and it was a grieving August song that did not end. The minutes were very long.

Frankie went again to the kitchen mirror and stared at her own face. 'The big mistake I made was to get this close crew-cut. For the wedding I ought to have long bright yellow hair. Don't you think so?'

She stood before the mirror and she was afraid. It was the summer of fear, for Frankie, and there was one fear that could be figured in arithmetic with paper and a pencil at the table. This August she was twelve and five-sixths years old. She was five feet five and three-quarter inches tall, and she wore a number seven shoe. In the past year she had grown four inches, or at least that was what she judged. Already the hateful little summer children hollered to her: 'Is it cold up there?' And the comments of grown people made

Frankie shrivel on her heels. If she reached her height on her eighteenth birthday, she had five and one-sixth growing years ahead of her. Therefore, according to mathematics and unless she could somehow stop herself, she would grow to be over nine feet tall. And what would be a lady who is over nine feet high? She would be a Freak.

In the early autumn of every year the Chattahoochee Exposition came to town. For a whole October week the fair went on down at the fair grounds. There was the Ferris Wheel, the Flying Jinney, the Palace of Mirrors – and there, too, was the House of the Freaks. The House of the Freaks was a long pavilion which was lined on the inside with a row of booths. It cost a quarter to go into the general tent, and you could look at each Freak in his booth. Then there were special private exhibitions farther back in the tent which cost a dime apiece. Frankie had seen all of the members of the Freak House last October:

The Giant
The Fat Lady
The Midget
The Wild Nigger
The Pin Head

The Alligator Boy
The Half-Man Half-Woman

The Giant was more than eight feet high, with huge loose hands and a hang-jaw face. The Fat Lady sat in a chair, and the fat on her was like loose-powdered dough which she kept slapping and working with her hands – next was the squeezed Midget who minced around in little trick evening clothes. The Wild Nigger came from a savage island. He squatted in his booth among the dusty bones and palm leaves and he ate raw living rats. The fair gave a free admission to his show to all who brought rats of the right size, and so children carried them down in strong sacks and shoe boxes. The Wild Nigger knocked the rat's head over his squatted knee and ripped off the fur and crunched and gobbled and flashed his greedy Wild Nigger eyes. Some said that he was not a genuine Wild Nigger, but a crazy coloured man from Selma. Anyway, Frankie did not like to watch him very long. She pushed through the crowd to the Pin-Head booth, where John Henry had stood all afternoon. The little Pin Head skipped and giggled and sassed around, with a shrunken head no larger than an orange, which was shaved except for one lock tied with a pink bow at the top. The last booth was always very crowded, for it was the booth of the Half-Man Half-Woman, a morphidite and a miracle of science. This Freak was divided completely in half – the left side was a man and the right side a woman. The costume on the left was a leopard skin and on the right side a brassiere and a spangled skirt. Half the face was dark-bearded and the other half bright glazed with paint. Both eyes were strange. Frankie had wandered around the tent and looked at every booth. She was afraid of all the Freaks, for it seemed to her that they had looked at her in a secret way and tried to connect their eyes with hers, as though to say: we know you. She was afraid of their long Freak eyes. And all the year she had remembered them, until this day.

'I doubt if they ever get married or go to a wedding,' she said. 'Those Freaks.'

'What freaks you talking about?' asked Berenice.

'At the fair,' said Frankie. 'The ones we saw there last October.'

'Oh, those folks.'

'I wonder if they make a big salary,' she said.

And Berenice answered: 'How would I know?'

John Henry held out an imaginary skirt and, touching his finger to the top of his big head, he skipped and danced like the Pin Head around the kitchen table.

Then he said: 'She was the cutest little girl I ever saw. I never saw anything so cute in my whole life. Did you, Frankie?'

'No,' she said. 'I didn't think she was cute.'

'Me and you both,' said Berenice.

'Shoo!' John Henry argued. 'She was, too.'

'If you want my candy opinion,' said Berenice, 'that whole crowd of folks down yonder at the fair just give me the creeps. Ever last one of them.'

Frankie watched Berenice through the mirror, and finally she asked in a slow voice. 'Do *I* give you the creeps?'

'You?' asked Berenice.

'Do you think I will grow into a Freak?' Frankie whispered.

'You?' said Berenice again. 'Why, certainly not, I trust Jesus.'

Frankie felt better. She looked sidewise at herself in the mirror. The clock ticked six slow times, and then she said: 'Well, do you think I will be pretty?

'Maybe. If you file down them horns a inch or two.'

Frankie stood with her weight resting on

her left leg, and she slowly shuffled the ball of her right foot on the floor. She felt a splinter go beneath the skin. 'Seriously,' she said.

'I think when you fill out you will do very well. If you behave.'

'But by Sunday,' Frankie said. 'I want to do something to improve myself before the wedding.'

'Get clean for a change. Scrub your elbows and fix yourself nice. You will do very well.'

Frankie looked for a last time at herself in the mirror, and then she turned away. She thought about her brother and the bride, and there was a tightness in her that would not break.

'I don't know what to do. I just wish I would die.'

'Well, die then!' said Berenice.

And: 'Die', John Henry echoed in a whisper.

The world stopped.

'Go home,' said Frankie to John Henry.

He stood with his big knees locked, his dirty little hand on the edge of the white table, and he did not move.

'You heard me,' Frankie said. She made a terrible face at him and grabbed the frying pan that hung above the stove. She chased him three times around the table, then up through the front hall and out of the door. She locked the front door and called again: 'Go home.'

'Now what makes you act like that?' asked Berenice. 'You are too mean to live.'

Frankie opened the door to the stairway that led up to her room, and sat down on one of the lower steps. The kitchen was silent and crazy and sad.

'I know it,' she said. 'I intend to sit still by myself and think over everything for a while.'

This was the summer when Frankie was sick and tired of being Frankie. She hated herself, and had become a loafer and a big no-good who hung around the summer kitchen: dirty and greedy and mean and sad. Besides being too mean to live, she was a criminal. If the Law knew about her, she could be tried in the courthouse and locked up in the jail. Yet Frankie had not always been a criminal and a big no-good. Until the April of that year, and all the years of her life before, she had been like other people. She belonged to a club and was in the seventh grade at school. She worked for her father on Saturday morning and went to the show every Saturday afternoon. She was not the kind of person ever to think of being afraid. At night she slept in the bed with her father, but not because she was scared of the dark.

Then the spring of that year had been a long queer season. Things began to change and Frankie did not understand this change. After the plain grey winter the March winds banged on the window-panes, and clouds were shirred and white on the blue sky. April that year came sudden and still, and the green of the trees was a wild bright green. The pale wisterias bloomed all over town, and silently the blossoms shattered. There was something about the green trees and the flowers of April that made Frankie sad. She did not know why she was sad, but because of this peculiar sadness, she began to realize she ought to leave the town. She read the war news and thought about the world and packed her suitcase to go away; but she did not know where she should go.

It was the year when Frankie thought about the world. And she did not see it as a round school globe, with the countries neat and different-coloured. She thought of the world as huge and cracked and loose and turning a thousand miles an hour. The geography book at school was out of date; the countries of the world had changed. Frankie read the war news in the paper, but there were so many foreign places, and the war was happening so fast, that sometimes she did not understand. It was the summer when Patton was chasing the Germans across France. And they were fighting, too, in Russia and Saipan. She saw the battles, and the soldiers. But there were too many different battles, and she could not see in her mind the millions and millions of soldiers all at once. She saw one Russian soldier, dark and frozen with a frozen gun, in Russian snow. The single Japs with slanted eyes on a jungle island gliding among green vines. Europe and the people hung in trees and the battleships on the blue oceans. Four-motor planes and burning cities and a soldier in a steel war helmet, laughing. Sometimes these pictures of the war, the world, whirled in her mind and she was dizzy. A long time ago she had predicted that it would take two months to win the whole war, but now she did not know. She wanted to be a boy and go to the war as a Marine. She thought about flying aeroplanes and winning gold medals for bravery. But she could not join the war, and this made her sometimes feel restless and blue. She decided to donate blood to the Red Cross; she wanted to donate a quart a week and her blood would be in the veins of Australians and Fighting French and Chinese, all over the whole world, and it would be as though she were close kin to all of these people. She could hear the army doctors saying that the blood of Frankie Addams was the reddest and the strongest blood that they had ever known. And she could picture ahead, in the years after the war, meeting the soldiers who had her blood, and they would say that they owed their life to her; and they would not call her Frankie – they would call her Addams. But this plan for donating her blood to the war did not come true. The Red Cross would not take her blood. She was too young. Frankie felt mad with the Red Cross, and left out of everything. The war and the world were too fast and big and strange. To think about the world for very long made her afraid. She was not afraid of Germans or bombs or Japanese. She was afraid because in the war they would not include her, and because the world seemed somehow separate from herself.

So she knew she ought to leave the town and go to some place far away. For the late spring, that year, was lazy and too sweet. The long afternoon flowered and lasted and the green sweetness sickened her. The town began to hurt Frankie. Sad and terrible happenings had never made Frankie cry, but this season many things made Frankie suddenly wish to cry. Very early in the morning she would sometimes go out into the yard and stand for a long time looking at the sunrise sky. And it was as though a question came into her heart, and the sky did not answer. Things she had never noticed much before began to hurt her: home lights watched from the evening sidewalks, an unknown voice from an alley. She would stare at the lights and listen to the voice, and something inside her stiffened and waited. But the lights would darken, the voice fall silent, and though she waited, that was all. She was afraid of these things that made her suddenly wonder who she was, and what she was going to be in the world, and why she was standing at that minute, seeing a light, or listening, or staring up into the sky: alone. She was afraid, and there was a queer tightness in her chest.

One night in April, when she and her father were going to bed, he looked at her and said, all of a sudden: 'Who is this great big long-legged twelve-year-old blunderbuss who still wants to sleep with her old Papa.' And she was too big to sleep with her father any more. She had to sleep in her upstairs room alone. She began to have a grudge against her father and they looked at each other in a slant-eyed way. She did not like to stay at home.

She went around town, and the things she saw and heard seemed to be left somehow unfinished, and there was the tightness in her that would not break. She would hurry to do something, but what she did was always wrong. She would call her best friend, Evelyn Owen, who owned a football suit and a Spanish shawl, and one would dress in the football suit and the other in the Spanish shawl and they would go down to the ten-cent store together. But that was a wrong thing and not what Frankie wanted. Or after the pale spring twilights, with the smell of dust and flowers sweet and bitter in the air, evenings of lighted windows and the long drawn calls at supper-time, when the chimney swifts had gathered and whirled above the town and flown off somewhere to their home together, leaving the sky empty and wide; after the long twilights of this season, when Frankie had walked around the sidewalks of the town, a jazz sadness quivered her nerves and her heart stiffened and almost stopped.

Because she could not break this tightness gathering within her, she would hurry to do something. She would go home and put the coal scuttle on her head, like a crazy

42

person's hat, and walk around the kitchen table. She would do anything that suddenly occurred to her – but whatever she did was always wrong, and not at all what she had wanted. Then, having done these wrong and silly things, she would stand, sickened and empty, in the kitchen door and say:

'I just wish I could tear down this whole town.'

'Well tear it down, then. But quit hanging around here with that gloomy face. Do something.'

And finally the troubles started.

She did things and got herself in trouble. She broke the law. And having once become a criminal, she broke the law again, and then again. She took the pistol from her father's bureau drawer and carried it all over town and shot up the cartridges in a vacant lot. She changed into a robber and stole a three-way knife from the Sears and Roebuck Store. One Saturday afternoon in May she committed a secret and unknown sin. In the MacKeans' garage, with Barney MacKean, they committed a queer sin, and how bad it was she did not know. The sin made a shrivelling sickness in her stomach, and she dreaded the eyes of everyone. She hated Barney and wanted to kill him. Sometimes alone in the bed at night she planned to shoot him with the pistol or throw a knife between his eyes.

Her best friend, Evelyn Owen, moved away to Florida, and Frankie did not play with anybody any more. The long and flowering spring was over and the summer in the town was ugly and lonesome and very hot. Every day she wanted more and more to leave the town: to light out for South America or Hollywood or New York City. But although she packed her suitcase many times, she could never decide to which of these places she ought to go, or how she would get there by herself.

So she stayed home and hung around the kitchen, and the summer did not end. By dog days she was five feet five and three-quarter inches tall, a great big greedy loafer who was too mean to live. She was afraid, but not as she had been before. There was only the fear of Barney, her father, and the Law. But even these fears were finally gone; after a long time the sin in the MacKeans' garage became far from her and was remembered only in her dreams. And she would not think of her father or the Law. She stuck close to the kitchen with John Henry and Berenice. She did not think about the war, the world. Nothing hurt her any longer; she did not care. She never stood alone in the back yard in order to stare up at the sky. She paid no attention to sounds and summer voices, and did not walk the streets of town at night. She would not let things make her sad and she would not care. She ate and wrote shows and practised throwing knives against the side of the garage and played bridge at the kitchen table. Each day was like the day before, except that it was longer, and nothing hurt her any more.

So that Friday when it happened, when her brother and the bride came to the house, Frankie knew that everything was changed; but why this was so, and what would happen to her next, she did not know. And though she tried to talk with Berenice, Berenice did not know either.

'It gives me this kind of pain,' she said, 'to think about them.'

'Well, don't,' said Berenice. 'You done nothing but think and carry on about them all this afternoon.'

Frankie sat on the bottom step of the stairs to her room, staring into the kitchen. But although it gave her a kind of a pain, she had to think about the wedding. She remembered the way her brother and the bride had looked when she walked into the living-room, that morning at eleven o'clock. There had been in the house a sudden silence, for Jarvis had turned off the radio when they came in; after the long summer, when the radio had gone on day and night, so that no one heard it any more, the curious silence had startled Frankie. She stood in the doorway, coming from the hall, and the first sight of her brother and the bride had shocked her heart. Together they made in her this feeling that she could not name. But it was like the feeling of the spring, only more sudden and more sharp. There was the same tightness and in the same queer way she was afraid. Frankie thought until her mind was dizzy and her foot had gone to sleep.

Then she asked Berenice: 'How old were you when you married your first husband?'

While Frankie was thinking, Berenice had changed into her Sunday clothes, and now she sat reading a magazine. She was waiting for the people who were due to meet her at six o'clock, Honey and T.T. Williams; the three of them were going to eat supper at the New Metropolitan Tea Room and sashay together around the town. As Berenice read, she moved her lips to shape each word. Her dark eye looked up as Frankie spoke, but, since Berenice did not raise her head, the blue glass eye seemed to go on reading the magazine. This two-sighted expression bothered Frankie.

'I were thirteen years old,' said Berenice.

'What made you get married so young for?'

'Because I wanted to,' said Berenice. 'I were thirteen years old and I haven't growed a inch since.'

Berenice was very short, and Frankie looked hard at her and asked: 'Does marrying really stop your growth?'

'It certainy do,' said Berenice.

'I didn't know that,' Frankie said.

Berenice had been married four different times. Her first husband was Ludie Freeman, a brickmason, and the favourite and best one of the four; he gave Berenice her fox fur, and once they had gone to Cincinnati and seen snow. Berenice and Ludie Freeman had seen a whole winter of Northern snow. They loved each other and were married for nine years, until the November he was sick and died. The other three husbands were all bad, each one worse than the one before, and it made Frankie blue just to hear about them. The first was a sorry old liquor-drinker. The next went crazy on Berenice: he did crazy things, had eating dreams in the night and swallowed a corner of the sheet; and what with one thing and another he distracted Berenice so much that finally she had to quit him. The last husband was terrible. He gouged out Berenice's eye and stole her furniture away from her. She had to call the Law on him.

'Did you marry with a veil every time?' asked Frankie.

'Two times with a veil,' said Berenice.

Frankie could not keep still. She walked around the kitchen, although there was a splinter in her right foot and she was limping, her thumbs hooked in the belt of her shorts and her undershirt clinging and wet.

Finally she opened the drawer of the kitchen table and selected a long sharp butcher knife. Then she sat down and rested the ankle of her sore foot on her left knee. The sole of her foot was long and narrow, pitted with ragged whitish scars, as every summer Frankie stepped on many nails; Frankie had the toughest feet in town. She could slice off waxy yellow rinds from the bottoms of her feet, and it did not hurt her very much, although it would hurt other people. But she did not chisel for the splinter immediately – she just sat there, her ankle on her knee and the knife in her right hand, looking across the table at Berenice.

'Tell me,' she said. 'Tell me exactly how it was.'

'You know!' said Berenice. 'You seen them.'

'But tell me,' Frankie said.

'I will discuss it for the last time,' said Berenice. 'Your brother and the bride come late this morning and you and John Henry hurried in from the back yard to see them. The next thing I realize you busted back through the kitchen and run up to your room. You came down with your organdie dress on and lipstick a inch thick from one ear to the next. Then you all just sat around up in the living-room. It was hot. Jarvis had brought Mr Addams a bottle of whisky and they had liquor drinks and you and John Henry had lemonade. Then after dinner your brother and the bride took the three o'clock train back to Winter Hill. The wedding will be this coming Sunday. And that is all. Now, is you satisfied?'

'I am so disappointed they couldn't stay longer – at least spend the night. After Jarvis being away so long. But I guess they want to be together as long as they can. Jarvis said he had some army papers to fill out at Winter Hill.' She took a deep breath. 'I wonder where they will go after the wedding.'

'On their honeymoon. Your brother will

have a few days' leave.'

'I wonder where that honeymoon will be.'

'Well, I'm sure I don't know.'

'Tell me,' Frankie said again. 'Exactly what did they look like?'

'Look like?' said Berenice. 'Why, they looked natural. Your brother is a good-looking blond white boy. And the girl is a kind of brunette and small and pretty. They make a nice white couple. You seen them, Foolish.'

Frankie closed her eyes, and, though she did not see them as a picture, she could feel them leaving her. She could feel the two of them together on the train, riding and riding away from her. They were them, and leaving her, and she was her, and sitting left all by herself there at the kitchen table. But a part of her was with them, and she could feel this part of her own self going away, and farther away; farther and farther, so that a drawn-out sickness came in her, going away and farther away, so that the kitchen Frankie was an old hull left there at the table.

'It is so queer,' she said.

She bent over the sole of her foot, and there was something wet, like tears or sweat drops, on her face; she sniffled and began to cut for the splinter.

'Don't that hurt you none?' asked Berenice.

Frankie shook her head and did not answer. Then after a moment she said: 'Have you ever seen any people that afterward you remembered more like a feeling than a picture?'

'How you mean?'

'I mean this,' said Frankie slowly. 'I saw them O.K. Janice had on a green dress and green high-heel dainty shoes. Her hair was done up in a knot. Dark hair and a little piece of it was loose. Jarvis sat by her on the sofa. He had on his brown uniform and he was sunburned and very clean. They were the two prettiest people I ever saw. Yet it was like I couldn't see all of them I wanted to see. My brain couldn't gather together quick enough and take it all in. And then they were gone. You see what I mean?'

'Your hurting yourself,' said Berenice. 'What you need is a needle.'

'I don't care anything about my old feet,' Frankie said.

It was only half past six, and the minutes of the afternoon were like bright mirrors. From outside there was no longer the sound of whistling and in the kitchen nothing moved. Frankie sat facing the door that opened on to the back porch. There was a square cat-hole cut in a corner of the back door, and nearby a saucer of lavender sour milk. In the beginning of dog days Frankie's cat had gone away. And the season of dog days is like this: it is the time at the end of the summer when as a rule nothing can happen – but if a change does come about, that change remains until dog days are over. Things that are done are not undone and a mistake once made is not corrected.

That August Berenice scratched a mosquito bite under her right arm and it became a sore: that sore would never heal until dog days were over. Two little families of August gnats picked out the corners of John Henry's eyes to settle down in, and though he often shook himself and blinked, those gnats were there to stay. Then Charles disappeared. Frankie did not see him leave the house and walk away, but on the fourteenth of August, when she called him to his supper, he did not come, and he was gone. She looked for him everywhere and sent John Henry wailing his name through all the streets of town. But it was the season of dog days and Charles did not come back again. Every afternoon Frankie said exactly the same words to Berenice, and the answers of Berenice were always the same. So that now the words were like an ugly little tune they sang by heart.

'If only I knew where he has gone.'

'Quit worrying yourself about that old alley cat. I done told you he ain't coming back.'

'Charles is not alley. He is almost pure Persian.'

'Persian as I is,' Berenice would say. 'You seen the last of that old tomcat. He gone off to hunt a friend.

'To hunt a friend?'

'Why, certainy. He roamed off to find himself a lady friend.'

'You really think so?'

'Naturally.'

'Well, why don't he bring his friend home with him? He ought to know I would be only too glad to have a whole family of cats.'

'You seen the last of that old alley cat.'

'If only I just knew where he is gone.'

And so each gloomy afternoon their voices sawed against each other, saying the same words, which finally reminded Frankie of the raggedy rhyme said by two crazies. She would end by telling Berenice: 'It looks to me like everything has just walked off and left me.' And she would put her head down on the table and feel afraid.

But this afternoon Frankie suddenly changed all this. An idea came to her, and she put down the knife and got up from the table.

'I know what I ought to do,' she suddenly said. 'Listen.'

'I can hear.'

'I ought to notify the police force. They will find Charles.'

'I wouldn't do that,' said Berenice.

Frankie went to the hall telephone and explained to the Law about her cat. 'He is almost pure Persian,' she said. 'But with short hair. A very lovely colour of grey with a little white spot on his throat. He answers to the name of *Charles*, but if he don't answer to that, he might come if you call *Charlina*. My name is Miss F. Jasmine Addams and the address is 124 Grove Street.'

Berenice was giggling when she came back, a soft high giggle. 'Whew! They going to send around here and tie you up and drag you off to Milledgeville. Them fat blue police chasing tomcats around alleys and hollering: *Oh Charles, Oh come here, Charlina!* Sweet Jesus!'

'Aw, shut up,' Frankie said.

Berenice was sitting at the table; she had stopped giggling and her dark eye roved in a teasing way as she sloshed coffee into a white china saucer to cool.

'At the same time,' she said, 'I can't see how it is such a wise idea to trifle around

54

with the Law. No matter for what reason.'

'I'm not trifling with the Law.'

'You just now set there and spelled them out your name and your house number. Where they can lay hold of you if ever they take the notion.'

'Well, let them!' said Frankie angrily. 'I don't care! I don't care!' And suddenly she did not care if anybody knew she was a criminal or not. 'Let them come get me for all I care.'

'I was just teasing you,' said Berenice. 'The trouble with you is that you don't have no sense of humour any more.'

'Maybe I'd be better off in jail.'

Frankie walked around the table and she could feel them going away. The train was travelling to the North. Mile after mile they went away, farther and farther away from the town, and as they travelled to the North, a coolness came into the air and dark was falling like the evening dark of wintertime. The train was winding up into the hills, the whistle wailing in a winter tone, and mile after mile they went away. They passed among themselves a box of bought store candy, with chocolates set in dainty, pleated shells, and watched the winter miles pass by the window. Now they had gone a long, long way from town and soon would be in Winter Hill.

'Sit down,' said Berenice. 'You make me nervous.'

Suddenly Frankie began to laugh. She wiped her face with the back of her hand and went back to the table. 'Did you hear what Jarvis said?'

'What?'

Frankie laughed and laughed.

'They were talking about whether to vote for C.P. MacDonald. And Jarvis said: *Why, I wouldn't vote for that scoundrel if he was running to be the dog-catcher.* I never heard anything so witty in my life.'

Berenice did not laugh. Her dark eye glanced down in a corner, quickly saw the joke, and then looked back at Frankie. Berenice wore her pink crêpe dress and her hat with the pink plume was on the table. The blue glass eye made the sweat on her dark face look bluish also. Berenice was stroking the hat plume with her hand.

'And you know what Janice remarked?' asked Frankie. 'When Papa mentioned about how much I've grown, she said she didn't think I looked so terribly big. She said she got the major portion of her growth before she was thirteen. She did, Berenice!'

'O.K.! All right.'

'She said she thought I was a lovely size and would probably not grow any taller. She said all fashion models and movie stars–'

'She did not,' said Berenice. 'I heard her. She only remarked that you probably had already got your growth. But she didn't go on and on like that. To hear you tell it, anybody would think she took her text on the subject.'

'She said–'

'This is a serious fault with you, Frankie. Somebody just makes a loose remark and then you cozen it in your mind until nobody would recognize it. Your Aunt Pet happened to mention to Clorina that you had sweet manners and Clorina passed it on to you. For what it was worth. The next thing I know you are going all round and bragging how Mrs West thought you had the finest manners in town and ought to go to Hollywood, and I don't know what all you didn't say. You keep building on to any little compliment you hear about yourself. Or, if it is a bad thing, you do the same. You cozen and change things too much in your own mind. And that is a serious fault.'

'Quit preaching at me,' Frankie said.

'I ain't preaching. It is the solemn truth.'

'I admit it a little,' said Frankie finally. She

closed her eyes and the kitchen was very quiet. She could feel the beating of her heart, and when she spoke her voice was a whisper. 'What I need to know is this. Do you think I made a good impression?'

'Impression? Impression?'

'Yes,' said Frankie, her eyes still closed.

'Well, how would I know?' said Berenice.

'I mean how did I act? What did I do?'

'Why, you didn't do anything.'

'Nothing?' asked Frankie.

'No. You just watched the pair of them like they was ghosts. Then, when they talked about the wedding, them ears of yours stiffened out the size of cabbage leaves—'

Frankie raised her hand to her left ear. 'They didn't,' she said bitterly. Then after a while she added, 'Some day you going to look down and find that big fat tongue of yours pulled out by the roots and laying there before you on the table. Then how do you think you will feel?'

'Quit talking so rude,' said Berenice.

Frankie scowled down at the splinter in her foot. She finished cutting it out with the knife and said, 'That would have hurt anybody else but me.' Then she was walking round and round the room again. 'I am so scared I didn't make a good impression.'

'What of it?' said Berenice. 'I wish Honey and T.T. would come on. You make me nervous.'

Frankie drew up her left shoulder and bit her lower lip. Then suddenly she sat down and banged her forehead on the table.

'Come on,' said Berenice. 'Don't act like that.'

But Frankie sat stiff, her face in the crook of her elbow and her fists clenched tight. Her voice had a ragged and strangled sound. 'They were so pretty,' she was saying. 'They must have such a good time. And they went away and left me.'

'Sit up,' said Berenice. 'Behave yourself.'

'They came and went away,' she said. 'They went away and left me with this feeling.'

'Hooee!' said Berenice finally. 'I bet I know something.'

The kitchen was silent and she tapped four times with her heel: one, two, three – *bang!* Her live eye was dark and teasing and she tapped with her heel, then took up the beating with a dark jazz voice that was like a song.

'Frankie got a crush!
Frankie got a crush!
Frankie got a crush!
'On the *Wedd*-ing!'

'Quit,' said Frankie.

'Frankie got a crush!
Frankie got a crush!'

Berenice went on and on, and her voice was jazzed like the heart that beats in your head when you have fever. Frankie was dizzy, and she picked up the knife from the kitchen table.

'You better quit!'

Berenice stopped very suddenly. The kitchen was suddenly shrunken and quiet.

'You lay down that knife.'

'Make me.'

She steadied the end of the handle against her palm and bent the blade slowly. The knife was limber, sharp, and long.

'Lay it down, DEVIL!'

But Frankie stood up and took careful aim. Her eyes were narrowed and the feel of the knife made her hands stop trembling.

'Just throw it!' said Berenice. 'You just!'

All the house was very quiet. The empty house seemed to be waiting. And then there was the knife whistle in the air and the sound the blade made when it struck. The knife hit the middle of the stairway door and shivered there. She watched the knife until it did not shiver any longer.

'I am the best knife-thrower in this town,' she said.

Berenice, who stood behind her, did not speak.

'If they would have a contest I would win.'

Frankie pulled the knife from the door and laid it on the kitchen table. Then she spat on her palm and rubbed her hands together.

Berenice said finally: 'Frances Addams, you going to do that once too often.'

'I never miss outside of a few inches.'

'You know what your father said about knife-throwing in this house.'

'I warned you to quit picking with me.'

'You are not fit to live in a house,' said Berenice.

'I won't be living in this one much longer. I'm going to run away from home.'

'And a good riddance to a big old bad rubbage,' said Berenice.

'You wait and see. I'm leaving town.'

'And where you think you are going?'

Frankie looked at all the corners of the room, and then said, 'I don't know.'

'I do,' said Berenice. 'You going crazy. That's where you going.'

'No,' said Frankie. She stood very still,

looking around the queerly pictured wall, and then she closed her eyes. 'I'm going to Winter Hill. I'm going to the wedding. And I swear to Jesus by my two eyes I'm never coming back here any more.'

She had not been sure that she would throw the knife until it struck and shivered on the stairway door. And she had not known that she would say these words until already they were spoken. The swear was like the sudden knife: she felt it strike in her and tremble. Then when the words were quiet, she said again:

'After the wedding I'm not coming back.'

Berenice pushed back the damp bangs of Frankie's hair and finally she asked: 'Sugar? You serious?'

'Of course!' said Frankie. 'Do you think I would stand here and swear that swear and tell a story? Sometimes, Berenice, I think it takes you longer to realize a fact than it does anybody who ever lived.'

'But,' said Berenice, 'you say you don't know where you're going. You going, but you don't know where. That don't make no sense to me.'

Frankie stood looking up and down the four walls of the room. She thought of the world, and it was fast and loose and turning, faster and looser and bigger than ever it had been before. The pictures of the War sprang out and clashed together in her mind. She saw bright flowered islands and a land by a northern sea with the grey waves on the shore. Bombed eyes and the shuffle of soldiers' feet. Tanks and a plane, wing broken, burning and downward falling in a desert sky. The world was cracked by the loud battles and turning a thousand miles a minute. The names of places spun in Frankie's mind: China, Peachville, New Zealand, Paris, Cincinnati, Rome. She thought of the huge and turning world until her legs began to tremble and there was sweat on the palms of her hands. But still she did not know where she should go. Finally she stopped looking around the four kitchen walls and said to Berenice:

'I feel just exactly like somebody has peeled all the skin off me. I wish I had some cold good chocolate ice cream.'

Berenice had her hands on Frankie's shoulders and was shaking her head and staring with the live eye narrowed into Frankie's face.

'But every word I told you was the solemn truth,' she said. 'I'm not coming back here after the wedding.'

There was a sound, and when they turned they saw that Honey and T.T. Williams were standing in the doorway. Honey, though he was her foster brother, did not resemble Berenice – and it was almost as though he came from some foreign country, like Cuba or Mexico. He was light-skinned, almost lavender in colour, with quiet narrow eyes like oil, and a limber body. Behind the two of them stood T.T. Williams, and he was very big and black; he was grey-haired, older even than Berenice, and he wore a church suit with a red badge in the buttonhole. T.T. Williams was a beau of Berenice, a well-off coloured man who owned a coloured restaurant. Honey was a sick, loose person. The army would not include him, and he had shovelled in a gravel pit until he broke one of his insides and could not do heavy work any more. They stood, the three of them, dark and grouped together in the door.

'What you all creep up like that for?' asked Berenice. 'I didn't even hear you.'

'You and Frankie too busy discussing something,' said T.T.

'I am ready to go,' said Berenice. 'I been ready. But do you wish a small little quickie before we start?'

T.T. Williams looked at Frankie and

shuffled his feet. He was very proper, and he liked to please everybody, and he always wanted to do the right thing.

'Frankie ain't no tattle-tale,' said Berenice. 'Is you?'

Frankie would not even answer such a question. Honey wore a dark red rayon slack suit and she said: 'That sure is a cute suit you got on, Honey. Where did you get it?'

Honey could talk like a white school-teacher; his lavender lips could move as quick and light as butterflies. But he only answered with a coloured word, a dark sound from the throat that can mean anything. 'Ahhnnh,' he said.

The glasses were before them on the table, and the hair-straightening bottle that held gin, but they did not drink. Berenice said something about Paris and Frankie had the extra feeling that they were waiting for her to leave. She stood in the door and looked at them. She did not want to go away.

'You wish water in yours, T.T?' asked Berenice.

They were together around the table and Frankie stood extra in the door alone. 'So long, you all,' she said.

''Bye, Sugar,' said Berenice. 'You forget all that foolishness we was discussing. And if

Mr Addams don't come home by dark, you go on over to the Wests. Go play with John Henry.'

'Since when have I been scared of the dark?' said Frankie. 'So long.'

'So long,' the said.

She closed the door, but behind her she could hear their voices. With her head against the kitchen door she could hear the murmuring dark sounds that rose and fell in a gentle way. Ayee – ayee. And then Honey spoke above the idle wash of voices and he asked: 'What was it between you and Frankie when we come in the house?' She waited, her ear pressed close against the door, to hear what Berenice would say. And finally the words were: 'Just foolishness. Frankie was carrying on with foolishness.' She listened until at last she heard them go away.

The empty house was darkening. She and her father were alone at night, as Berenice went to her own home directly after supper. Once they had rented the front bedroom. It was the year after her grandmother died, when Frankie was nine. They rented the front bedroom to Mr and Mrs Marlowe. The only thing Frankie remembered about them was the remark said at the last, that they were common people. Yet for the season they were there, Frankie was fascinated by Mr and Mrs Marlowe and the front room. She loved to go in when they were away and carefully, lightly meddle with their things – with Mrs Marlowe's atomizer which skeeted perfume, the grey-pink powder puff, the wooden shoe-trees of Mr Marlowe. They left mysteriously after an afternoon that Frankie did not understand. It was a summer Sunday and the hall door of the Marlowes' room was open. She could see only a portion of the room, part of the dresser and only the footpiece of the bed with Mrs Marlowe's corset on it. But there was a sound in the quiet room she could not place, and when she stepped over the threshold she was startled by a sight that, after a single glance, sent her running to the kitchen, crying: Mr Marlowe is having a fit. Berenice had hurried through the hall, but when she looked into the front room, she merely bunched her lips and banged the door. And evidently told her father, for that evening he said the Marlowes would have to leave. Frankie had tried to question Berenice and find out what was the matter. But Berenice had only said that they were common people and added that with a certain party in the house they ought at least to know enough to shut a door. Though Frankie knew she was the certain party, still she did not understand. What kind of a fit was it? she asked. But Berenice would only answer: Baby, just a common fit. And Frankie knew from the voice's tones that there was more to it than she was told. Later she only remembered the Marlowes as common people, and being common they owned common things – so that long after she had ceased to think about the Marlowes or fits, remembering merely the name and the fact that once they had rented the front bedroom, she associated common people with grey-pink powder puffs and perfume atomizers. The front bedroom had not been rented since.

Frankie went to the hall hat rack and put on one of her father's hats. She looked at her dark ugly mug in the mirror. The conversation about the wedding had somehow been wrong. The questions she had asked that afternoon had all been the wrong questions, and Berenice had answered her with jokes. She could not name the feeling in her, and she stood there until dark shadows made her think of ghosts.

Frankie went out to the street before the house and looked up into the sky. She stood staring with her fist on her hip and her mouth open. The sky was lavender and slowly darkening. She heard in the neighbourhood the sound of evening voices and noticed the light fresh smell of watered grass. This was the time of the early evening when, since the kitchen was too hot, she would go for a little while outdoors. She practised knife-throwing, or sat before the cold-drink store in the front yard. Or she would go around to the back yard, and there the arbour was cool and dark. She wrote shows, although she had outgrown all of her costumes, and was too big to act in them beneath the arbour; this summer she had written very cold shows – shows about Eskimos and frozen explorers. Then when night had come she would go again back in the house.

But this evening Frankie did not have her mind on knives or cold-drink stores or shows. Nor did she want to stand there staring up into the sky; for her heart asked the old questions, and in the old way of the spring she was afraid.

She felt she needed to think about something ugly and plain, so she turned from the evening sky and stared at her own house. Frankie lived in the ugliest house in town, but now she knew that she would not be living there much longer. The house was empty, dark. Frankie turned and walked to the end of the block, and around the corner, and down the sidewalk to the Wests'. John Henry was leaning against the banisters of his front porch, with a lighted window behind him, so that he looked like a little black paper doll on a piece of yellow paper.

'Hey,' she said. 'I wonder when that Papa of mine is coming home from town.'

John Henry did not answer.

'I don't want to go back in that dark old ugly house all my myself.'

She stood on the sidewalk, looking at John Henry, and the smart political remark came back to her. She hooked her thumbs in the pockets of her pants and asked: 'If you were going to vote in an election, who would you vote for?'

John Henry's voice was bright and high in the summer night. 'I don't know,' he said.

'For instance, would you cast your vote for C.P. MacDonald to be mayor of this town?'

John Henry did not answer.

'Would you?'

But she could not get him to talk. There were times when John Henry would not answer anything you said to him. So she had to remark without an argument behind her, and all by herself like that it did not sound

70

very smart: 'Why, I wouldn't vote for him if he was running to be dog-catcher.'

The darkening town was very quiet. For a long time now her brother and the bride had been at Winter Hill. They had left the town a hundred miles behind them, and now were in a city far away. They were them and in Winter Hill, together, while she was her and in the same old town all by herself. The long hundred miles did not make her sadder and make her feel more far away than the knowing that they were them and both together and she was only her and parted from them, by herself. And as she sickened with this feeling a thought and explanation suddenly came to her, so that she knew and almost said aloud: *They are the we of me.* Yesterday, and all the twelve years of her life, she had only been Frankie. She was an *I* person who had to walk around and do things by herself. All other people had a *we* to claim, all other except her. When Berenice said *we,* she meant Honey and Big Mama, her lodge, or her church. The *we* of her father was the store. All members of clubs have a *we* to belong to and talk about. The soldiers in the army can say *we,* and even the criminals on chain-gangs. But the old Frankie had had no *we* to claim, unless it would be the terrible summer *we* of her and John Henry and Berenice – and that was the last *we* in the world she wanted. Now all this was suddenly over with and changed. There was her brother and the bride, and it was as though when first she saw them something she had known inside of her: *They are the we of me.* And that was why it made her feel so queer, for them to be away in Winter Hill while she was left all by herself; the hull of the old Frankie left there in the town alone.

'Why are you all bent over like that?' John Henry called.

'I think I have a kind of pain,' said Frankie. 'I must have ate something.'

John Henry was still standing on the banisters, holding to the post.

'Listen,' she said finally. 'Suppose you come on over and eat super and spend the night with me.'

'I can't,' he answered.

'Why?'

John Henry walked across the banisters, holding out his arms for balance, so that he was like a little blackbird against the yellow window light. He did not answer until he safely reached the other post.

'Just because.'

'Because why?'

He did not say anything, and so she added: 'I thought maybe me and you could put up my Indian tepee and sleep out in the back yard. And have a good time.'

Still John Henry did not speak.

'We're blood first cousins. I entertain you all the time. I've given you so many presents.'

Quietly, lightly, John Henry walked back across the banisters and then stood looking out at her with his arm around the post again.

'Sure enough,' she called. 'Why can't you come?'

At last he said. 'Because, Frankie, I don't want to.'

'Fool jackass!' she screamed. 'I only asked you because I thought you looked so ugly and so lonesome.'

Lightly John Henry jumped down from the banisters. And his voice as he called back to her was a clear child's voice.

'Why, I'm not a bit lonesome.'

Frankie rubbed the wet palms of her hands along the sides of her shorts and said in her mind: Now turn around and take yourself on home. But in spite of this order, she was somehow unable to turn around and go. It was not yet night. Houses along the street were dark, lights showed in windows.

Darkness had gathered in the thick-leaved trees and shapes in the distance were ragged and grey. But the night was not yet in the sky.

'I think something is wrong,' she said. 'It is too quiet. I have a peculiar warning in my bones. I bet you a hundred dollars it's going to storm.'

John Henry watched her from behind the banister.

'A terrible terrible dog day storm. Or maybe even a cyclone.'

Frankie stood waiting for the night. And just at that moment a horn began to play. Somewhere in the town, not far away, a horn began a blues tune. The tune was grieving and low. It was the sad horn of some coloured boy, but who he was she did not know. Frankie stood stiff, her head bent and her eyes closed, listening. There was something about the tune that brought back to her all of the spring: flowers, the eyes of strangers, rain.

The tune was low and dark and sad. Then all at once, as Frankie listened, the horn danced into a wild jazz spangle that zigzagged upward with sassy nigger trickiness. At the end of the jazz spangle the music rattled thin and far away. Then the tune returned to the first blues song, and it was like the telling of that long season of trouble. She stood there on the dark sidewalk and the drawn tightness of her heart made her knees lock and her throat feel stiffened. Then, without warning, the thing happened that at first Frankie could not believe. Just at the time when the tune should be laid, the music finished, the horn broke off. All of a sudden the horn stopped playing. For a moment Frankie could not take it in, she felt so lost.

She whispered finally to John Henry West: 'He has stopped to bang the spit out of his horn. In a second he will finish.'

But the music did not come again. The tune was left broken, unfinished. And the drawn tightness she could no longer stand. She felt she must do something wild and sudden that never had been done before. She hit herself on the head with her fist, but that did not help any at all. And she began to talk aloud, although at first she paid no attention to her own words and did not know in advance what she would say.

'I told Berenice that I was leaving town for good and she did not believe me. Sometimes I honestly think she is the biggest fool that ever drew breath.' She complained aloud, and her voice was fringed and sharp like the edge of a saw. She talked and did not know from one word to the next what she would say. She listened to her own voice, but the words she heard did not make much sense. 'You try to impress something on a big fool like that and it's just like talking to a block of cement. I kept on telling and telling and telling her. I told her I had to leave this town for good because it is inevitable.'

She was not talking to John Henry. She did not see him any more. He had moved from the lighted window, but he was still listening from the porch, and after a little while he asked her:

'Where?'

Frankie did not answer. She was suddenly very still and quiet. For a new feeling had come to her. The sudden feeling was that she knew deep in her where she would go. She knew, and in another minute the name of the place would come to her. Frankie bit the knuckles of her fist and waited: but she did not hunt the name of the place and did not think about the turning world. She saw in her mind her brother and the bride, and the heart in her was squeezed so hard that Frankie almost felt it break.

John Henry was asking in his high child voice: 'You want me to eat supper and sleep in the tepee with you?'

She answered: 'No.'

'You just a little while ago invited me!'

But she could not argue with John Henry West or answer anything he said. For it was just at that moment that Frankie understood. She knew who she was and how she was going into the world. Her squeezed heart suddenly opened and divided. Her heart divided like two wings. And when she spoke her voice was sure.

'I know where I'm going,' she said.

He asked her: 'Where?'

'I'm going to Winter Hill,' she said. 'I'm going to the wedding.'

She waited, to give him a chance to say: 'I already knew that, anyhow.' Then finally she spoke the sudden truth aloud.

'I'm going with them. After the wedding at Winter Hill, I'm going off with the two of them to whatever place that they will ever go. I'm going with them.'

He did not answer.

'I love the two of them so much. We'll go to every place together. It's like I've known it all my life, that I belong to be with them. I love the two of them so much.'

And having said this, she did not need to wonder and puzzle any more. She opened her eyes, and it was night. The lavender sky had at last grown dark and there was slanted starlight and twisted shade. Her heart had divided like two wings and she had never seen a night so beautiful.

Frankie stood looking into the sky. For when the old question came to her – the who she was and what she would be in the world, and why she was standing there that minute – when the old question came to her, she did not feel hurt and unanswered. At last she knew just who she was and understood where she was going. She loved her brother and the bride and she was a member of the wedding. The three of them would go into the world and they would always be together. And finally, after the scared spring and the crazy summer, she was no more afraid.

PART II

1

The day before the wedding was not like any day that F. Jasmine had ever known. It was the Saturday she went into the town, and suddenly, after the closed blank summer, the town opened before her and in a new way she belonged. Because of the wedding, F. Jasmine felt connected with all she saw, and it was as a sudden member that on this Saturday she went around the town. She walked the streets entitled as a queen and mingled everywhere. It was the day when, from the beginning, the world seemed no longer separate from herself and when all at once she felt included. Therefore, many things began to happen – nothing that came about surprised F. Jasmine and, until the last at least, all was natural in a magic way.

At the country house of an uncle of John Henry, Uncle Charles, she had seen old blindered mules going round and round in the same circle, grinding juice from the sugar cane for syrup. In the sameness of her tracks that summer, the old Frankie had somehow resembled that country mule; in town she browsed around the counters of the ten-cent store, or sat on the front row of the Palace show, or hung around her father's store, or stood on street corners watching soldiers. Now this morning was altogether different. She went into places she had never dreamed of entering until that day. For one thing, F. Jasmine went to a hotel – it was not the finest hotel in the town, or even the next to the finest, but nevertheless it was a hotel and F. Jasmine was there. Furthermore, she was there with a soldier, and that, too, was an unforeseen event, as she had never in her life laid eyes on him until that day. Only yesterday, if the old Frankie had glimpsed a boxlike vision of this scene, as a view seen through a wizard's periscope, she would have bunched her mouth with unbelief. But it was a morning when many things occurred, and a curious fact about this day was a twisted sense of the astonishing; the unexpected did not make her wonder, and only the long known, the familiar, struck her with strange surprise.

The day began when she waked up at dawn, and it was as though her brother and the bride had, in the night, slept on the bottom of her heart, so that the first instant she recognized the wedding. Next, and immediately, she thought about the town. Now that she was leaving home she felt in a curious way as though on this last day the town called to her and was now waiting. The windows of her room were cool dawn-blue. The old cock at the MacKeans' was crowing. Quickly she got up and turned on the bed lamp and the motor.

It was the old Frankie of yesterday who had been puzzled, but F. Jasmine did not wonder any more; already she felt familiar with the wedding for a long, long time. The black dividing night has something to do with this. In the twelve years before, whenever a sudden change had come about there was a certain doubt during the time when it was happening; but after sleeping through a night, and on the very next day, the change did not seem so sudden after all. Two summers past, when she had travelled with the Wests to Port Saint Peter on the bay, the first sea evening with the scalloped grey ocean and empty sand was to her like a foreign place, and she had gone around with slanted eyes and put her hands on things in doubt. But after the first night, as soon as she awoke next day, it was as though she had known Port Saint Peter all her life. Now it was likewise with the wedding. No longer questioning, she turned to other things.

She sat at her desk wearing only the blue-and-white striped trousers of her pyjamas which were rolled up above the knees, vibrating her right foot on the ball of her bare foot, and considering all that she must do on this last day. Some of these things she could name to herself, but there were other things that could not be counted on her fingers or made into a list with words. To start with, she decided to make herself some visiting cards with *Miss F. Jasmine Addams, Esq.,* engraved with squinted letters on a tiny card. So she put on her green visor eyeshade, cut up some cardboard, and fitted ink pens behind both ears. But her mind was restless and zigzagged to other things, and soon she began to get ready for town. She dressed carefully that morning in her most grown and best, the pink organdie, and put on lipstick and Sweet Serenade. Her father, a very early riser, was stirring in the kitchen when she went downstairs.

'Good morning, Papa.'

Her father was Royal Quincy Addams and he owned a jewellery store just off the main

82

street of the town. He answered her with a kind of grunt, for he was a grown person who liked to drink three cups of coffee before he started conversation for the day; he deserved a little peace and quiet before he put his nose down to the grindstone. F. Jasmine had heard him bungling about his room when once she waked up to drink water in the night, and his face was pale as cheese this morning, his eyes had a pink and ragged look. It was a morning when he despised a saucer because his cup would rattle against it and not fit, so he put his cup down on the table or stove top until brown circles were left all over everywhere and flies settled in quiet rings. There was some sugar spilt on the floor, and each time his step made a gritty sound his face shivered. This morning he wore a pair of saggy-kneed grey trousers and a blue shirt unfastened at the collar and with the tie loose. Since June she had had this secret grudge against him that almost she did not admit – since the night he had asked who was the great big blunderbuss who still wanted to sleep with her old Papa – but now she had this grudge no longer. All of a sudden it seemed to F. Jasmine that she saw her father for the first time, and she did not see him only as he was at that one minute, but pictures of the old days swirled in her mind and crossed each other. Remembrance, changing and fast, made F. Jasmine stop very still and stand with her head cocked, watching him both in the actual room and from somewhere inside her. But there were things that must be said, and when she spoke her voice was not unnatural.

'Papa, I think I ought to tell you now. I'm not coming back here after the wedding.'

He had ears to hear with, loose large ears with lavender rims, but he did not listen. He was a widowman, for her mother had died the very day that she was born – and, as a widowman, set in his ways. Sometimes, especially in the early morning, he did not listen to things she said or new suggestions. So she sharpened her voice and chiselled the words into his head.

'I have to buy a wedding dress and some wedding shoes and a pair of pink, sheer stockings.'

He heard, and after a consideration, gave her a permission nod. The grits boiled slowly with blue gluey bubbles, and as she set the table, she watched him and remembered. There were the winter mornings with frost flowers on the window-panes and the roaring stove and the look of his brown crusty hand as he leaned over her shoulder to help with a hard part of the last-minute arithmetic that she was working at the table, his voice explaining. Blue long spring evenings, she saw also, and her father on the dark front porch with his feet propped on the banisters, drinking the frosted bottles of beer he had sent her to bring home from Finny's Place. She saw him bent over the workbench down at the store, dipping a tiny spring in gasoline, or whistling and peering with his round jeweller's glass into a watch. Remembrances came sudden and swirled, each coloured with its own season, and for the first time she looked back on all the twelve years of her life and thought of them from a distance as a whole.

'Papa,' she said, 'I will write you letters.'

Now he walked the dawn-stale kitchen like a person who has lost something, but has forgotten what it is that he has lost. Watching him, the old grudge was forgotten, and she felt sorry. He would miss her in the house all by himself when she was gone. He would be lonesome. She wanted to speak some sorry words and love her father, but just at that moment he cleared his throat in the special way he used when he was going to lay down the law to her and said:

'Will you please tell me what has become of the monkey-wrench and screw-driver that were in my tool chest on the back porch?'

'The monkey-wrench and screw-driver–' F. Jasmine stood with her shoulders hunched, her left foot drawn up to the calf of the right leg. 'I borrowed them, Papa.'

'Where are they now?'

F. Jasmine considered. 'Over at the Wests'.'

'Now pay attention and listen to me,' her father said, holding the spoon that had been stirring the grits, and shaking it to mark the words. 'If you don't have the sense and judgement to leave things alone–' He stared at her in a long and threatening way, and finished: 'You'll have to be taught. From now on you walk the chalkline. Or you'll have to be taught.' He sniffed suddenly. 'Is that toast burning?'

It was still early in the morning when F. Jasmine left the house that day. The soft grey of the dawn had lightened and the sky was the wet pale blue of a watercolour sky just painted and not yet dried. There was a freshness in the bright air and cool dew on the burnt brown grass. From a back yard down the street, F. Jasmine could hear children's voices. She heard the calling voices of the neighbourhood children who were trying to

86

dig a swimming pool. They were all sizes and ages, members of nothing, and in the summers before, the old Frankie had been like leader or president of the swimming-pool diggers in that part of town – but now that she was twelve years old, she knew in advance that, though they would work and dig in various yards, not doubting to the very last the cool clear swimming pool of water, it would all end in a big wide ditch of shallow mud.

Now, as F. Jasmine crossed her yard, she saw in her mind's eye the swarming children and heard from down the street their chanting cries – and this morning, for the first time in her life, she heard a sweetness in these sounds, and she was touched. And, strange to say, her own home yard which she had hated touched her a little too; she felt she had not seen it for a long time. There, under the elm tree was her old cold-drink store, a light packing case that could be dragged around according to the shade, with a sign reading, DEW DROP INN. It was the time of morning when, the lemonade in a bucket underneath the store, she used to settle herself with her bare feet on the counter and the Mexican hat tilted down over her face – her eyes closed, smelling the strong smell of sun-warmed straw, waiting. And sometimes there would be customers and she would send John Henry to the A.&P. to buy some candy, but other times the Tempter Satan got the best of her and she drank up all the stock instead. But now this morning the store looked very small and staggered, and she knew that she would never run it any more. F. Jasmine thought of the whole idea as something over and done with that had happened long ago. A sudden plan came to her: after tomorrow, when she was with Janice and Jarvis, in the far place where they would be, she would look back on the old days and – But this was a plan F. Jasmine did not finish, for, as the names lingered in her mind, the gladness of the wedding rose up inside her and, although the day was an August day, she shivered.

The main street, too, seemed to F. Jasmine like a street returned to after many years, although she had walked up and down it only Wednesday. There were the same brick stores, about four blocks of them, the big white bank, and in the distance the many-windowed cotton mill. The wide street was divided by a narrow aisle of grass on either side of which the cars drove slowly in a browsing way. The glittering grey sidewalks and passing people, the striped awning over the stores, all was the same – yet, as she walked the street that morning, she felt free as a traveller who had never seen the town before.

And that was not all; she had no sooner walked down the left side of the main street and up again on the right sidewalk, when she realized a further happening. It had to do with various people, some known to her and others strangers, she met and passed along the street. An old coloured man, stiff and proud on his rattling wagon seat, drove a sad blindered mule down towards the Saturday market. F. Jasmine looked at him, he looked at her, and to the outward appearance that was all. But in that glance, F. Jasmine felt between his eyes and her own eyes a new unnameable connexion, as though they were known to each other – and there even came an instant vision of his home field and country roads and quiet dark pine trees as the wagon rattled past her on the paved town street. And she wanted him to know her, too – about the wedding.

Now the same thing happened again and again on those four blocks: with a lady going into MacDougal's store, with a small man waiting for the bus before the big First

National Bank, with a friend of her father's called Tut Ryan. It was a feeling impossible to explain in words – and later when she tried to tell of it at home Berenice raised up her eyebrows and dragged the word in a mocking way: Connexion? Connexion? But nevertheless it was there, this feeling – a connexion close as answers to calls. Furthermore, on the sidewalk before the First National Bank she found a dime and any other day that would have been a grand surprise, but now this morning she only paused to shine the dime on her dress front and put it in her pink pocketbook. Under the fresh blue early sky the feeling as she walked along was one of newly risen lightness, power, entitlement.

It was in a place called the Blue Moon that she first told about the wedding, and she came to the Blue Moon in a roundabout way, as it was not on the main street, but on the street called Front Avenue which bordered the river. She was in this neighbourhood because she had heard the organ of the monkey and the monkey-man and had set out immediately to find them. She had not seen the monkey and the monkey-man through the whole summer and it seemed a sign to her that she should run across them on this last day in town. She had not seen them for so long that sometimes she thought the pair of them might even be dead. They did not go around the streets in wintertime, for the cold wind made them sick; they went South in October to Florida and came back to town in warm late spring.

They, the monkey and the monkey-man, wandered to other towns also – but the old Frankie would come across them on various shaded streets through all the summers she could remember, except this one. He was a darling little monkey, and the monkey-man was nice also; the old Frankie had always loved them, and now she was dying to tell her plans and let them know about the wedding. So, when she first heard the broken-sounding, faint organ, she went at once in search of it, and the music seemed to come from near the river on Front Avenue. So she turned from the main street and hurried down the side street, but just before she reached Front Avenue the organ stopped, and when she gazed up and down the avenue she could not see the monkey or the monkey-man and all was silent and they were nowhere in sight. They had stopped, maybe, in a doorway or a shop – so F. Jasmine walked slowly with a watchful air.

Front Avenue was a street that had always

drawn her, although it had the sorriest, smallest stores in town. On the left side of the street there were warehouses, and in between were glimpses of brown river and green trees. On the right side there was a place with a sign reading Prophylactic Military, the business of which had often puzzled her, then other various places: a smelly fish shop with the shocked eyes of a single fish staring from some crushed ice in the window, a pawn-shop, a second-hand clothing store with out-of-style garments hanging from the narrow entrance and a row of broken shoes lined up on the sidewalk outside. Then finally there was the place called the Blue Moon. The street itself was cobbled with brick and angry-looking in the glare, and along the gutter she passed some eggshells and rotten lemon peels. It was not a fine street, but nevertheless the old Frankie had liked to come here now and then at certain times.

The street was quiet in the mornings and on the weekday afternoons. But towards evening, or on holidays, the street would fill with the soldiers who came from the camp nine miles away. They seemed to prefer Front Avenue to almost any other street, and some-times the pavement resembled a flowing river of brown soldiers. They came to town on holidays and went around in glad, loud gangs together, or walked the sidewalks with grown girls. And the old Frankie had always watched them with a jealous heart; they came from all over the whole country and were soon going all over the world. They went around in gangs together, those lasting twilights of the summertime – while the old Frankie dressed in her khaki shorts and Mexican hat watched from a distance by herself. Noises and weathers of distant places seemed to hover about them in the air. She imagined the many cities that these soldiers came from, and thought of the countries where they would go – while she was stuck there in the town forever. And stealing jealousy sickened her heart. But now this morning her heart was occupied with one intention: to tell of the wedding and her plans. So, after walking down the burning pavement, hunting for the monkey and the monkey-man, she came to the Blue Moon and it occurred to her that maybe they were there.

The Blue Moon was a place at the end of Front Avenue, and often the old Frankie had stood out on the sidewalk with her palms and nose pressed flat against the screen door, watching all that went on there. Customers, most of them soldiers, sat at the boothed tables, or stood at the counter having drinks, or crowded around the juke-box. Here sometimes there were sudden commotions. Late one afternoon when she passed the Blue Moon, she heard wild angry voices and a sound like a bottle being thrown, and as she stood there a policeman came out on the sidewalk pushing and jerking a torn-looking man with wobbly legs. The man was crying, shouting; there was blood on his ripped shirt and dirty tears dripped down his face. It was an April afternoon of rainbow showers, and by and by the Black Maria screamed down the street, and the poor arrested criminal was thrown into the prisoners' cage and carried off down to the jail. The old Frankie knew the Blue Moon well, although she had never been inside. There was no written law to keep her out, no lock and chain on the screen door. But she had known in an unworded way that it was a forbidden place to children. The Blue Moon was a place for holiday soldiers and the grown and free. The old Frankie had known she had no valid right to enter there, so she had only hung around the edges and never once had she gone inside. But now this morning before the wedding all of this was changed. The old laws she had known before meant nothing to F. Jasmine, and without a second thought she left the street and went inside.

There in the Blue Moon was the red-headed soldier who was to weave in such an unexpected way through all that day before the wedding. F. Jasmine, however, did not notice him at first; she looked for the monkey-man, but he was not there. Aside from the soldier the only other person in the room was the Blue Moon owner, a Portuguese, who stood behind the counter. This was the person F. Jasmine picked to be the first to hear about the wedding, and he was chosen simply because he was the one most likely and near.

After the fresh brightness of the street, the Blue Moon seemed dark. Blue neon lights burned over the dim mirror behind the counter, tinting the faces in the place pale green, and an electric fan turned slowly so that the room was scalloped with warm stale waves of breeze. At that early morning hour the place was very quiet. There were booth tables across the room, all empty. At the back of the Blue Moon a lighted wooden stairway led up to the second floor. The place smelled of dead beer and morning coffee. F. Jasmine ordered coffee from the owner behind the counter, and after he had brought it to her, he sat down on a stool across from her. He was a sad, pale man with a very flat face. He wore a long white apron and, hunched on the stool with his feet on the rungs, he was reading a romance magazine. The telling of the wedding gathered inside her, and when it was so ready she could no longer resist, she hunted in her mind a good opening remark – something grown and off-hand, to start between them the conversation. She said in a voice that trembled a little: 'It certainly has been an unseasonable summer, hasn't it?'

The Portuguese at first did not seem to hear her and went on reading the romance magazine. So she repeated her remark, and when his eyes were turned to hers and his attention caught, she went on in a higher voice: 'Tomorrow this brother of mine and his bride are marrying at Winter Hill.' She went straight to the story, as a circus dog breaks through the paper hoop, and as she talked, her voice became clearer, more definite, and sure. She told her plans in a way that made them sound completely settled, and not in the least open to question. The Portuguese listened with his head cocked to one side, his dark eyes ringed with ash-grey circles, and now and then he wiped his damp veined dead-white hands on his stained apron. She told about the wedding and her plans and he did not dispute with her or doubt.

It is far easier, it came to her as she remembered Berenice, to convince strangers of the coming to pass of dearest wants than those in your own home kitchen. The thrill of speaking certain words – Jarvis and Janice, wedding and Winter Hill – was such that F. Jasmine, when she had finished, wanted to start all over again. The Portuguese took from behind his ear a cigarette which he tapped on the counter but did not light. In the unnatural neon glow his face looked startled, and when she had finished he did not speak. With the telling of the wedding still sounding inside her, as the last chord of a guitar murmurs a long time after the strings are struck, F. Jasmine turned towards the entrance and the framed blazing street beyond the door: dark people passed along the sidewalk and footsteps echoed in the Blue Moon.

'It gives me a funny feeling,' she said. 'After living in this town all my whole life, to know that after tomorrow I'll never be back here any more.'

It was then she noticed him for the first time, the soldier who at the very end would twist so strangely that last, long day. Later, on thinking back, she tried to recall some warning hint of future craziness – but at the time he looked to her like any other soldier standing at a counter drinking beer. He was not tall, nor short, nor fat, nor thin – except for the red hair there was nothing at all unusual about him. He was one of the thousands of soldiers who came to the town from the camp nearby. But as she looked into this soldier's eyes, in the dim light of the Blue Moon, she realized that she gazed at him in a new way.

That morning, for the first time, F. Jasmine was not jealous. He might have come from New York or California – but she did not envy him. He might be on his way to England or India – she was not jealous. In the restless spring and crazy summer, she had watched the soldiers with a sickened heart, for they were the ones who came and went, while she was stuck there in the town forever. But now, on this day before the wedding, all this was changed; her eyes as she looked into the soldier's eyes were clear of jealousy and want. Not only did she feel that unexplainable connexion she was to feel between herself and other total strangers of that day, there was another sense of recognition: it seemed to F. Jasmine they exchanged the special look of friendly, free travellers who meet for a moment at some stop along the way. The look was long. And with the lifting of the jealous weight, F. Jasmine felt at peace. It was quiet in the Blue Moon, and the telling of the wedding seemed still to murmur in the room. After this long gaze of fellow travellers, it was the soldier who finally turned his face away.

'Yes,' said F. Jasmine, after a moment and to no one in particular, 'it gives me a mighty funny feeling. In a way it's like I ought to do all the things I would have done if I was staying in the town forever. Instead of this one day. So I guess I better get a move on. Adios.' She spoke the last word to the Portuguese, and at the same time her hand reached automatically to lift the Mexican hat she had worn all summer until that day, but, finding nothing, the gesture withered and her hand felt shamed. Quickly she scratched her head, and with a last glance at the soldier, left the Blue Moon.

It was the morning different from all other mornings she had ever known because of several reasons. First, of course, there was the telling of the wedding. Once, and a long time ago, the old Frankie had liked to go around the town playing a game. She had walked all around – through the north side of town with the grass-lawned houses and the sad mills section and coloured Sugarville – wearing her Mexican hat and the high-laced boots and a cowboy rope tied round her waist, she had gone around pretending to be Mexican. Me no speak English – Adios Buenos Noches – abla pokie peekie poo, she had jabbered in mock Mexican. Sometimes a little crowd of children gathered and the old Frankie would swell up with pride and trickery – but when the game was over, and she was home, there would come over her a cheated discontent. Now this morning reminded her of those old days of the Mexican game. She went to the same places, and the people, mostly strangers to her, were the same. But this morning she was not trying to trick people and pretend; far from it, she wanted only to be recognized for her true self. It was a need so strong, this want to be known and recognized, that F. Jasmine forgot the wild hard glare and choking dust and miles (it must have been at least five miles) of wandering all over town.

A second fact about that day was the forgotten music that sprang suddenly into her mind – snatches of orchestra minuets, march tunes, and waltzes, and the jazz horn of Honey Brown – so that her feet in the patent-leather shoes stepped always according to the tune. A last difference about that morning was the way her world seemed layered in three different parts, all the twelve years of the old Frankie, the present day itself, and the future ahead when the J A three of them would be together in all the many distant places.

As she walked along, it seemed as though the ghost of the old Frankie, dirty and hungry-eyed, trudged silently along not far from her, and the thought of the future, after the wedding, was constant as the very sky. That day alone seemed equally important as both the long past and the bright future – as a hinge is important to a swinging door. And since it was the day when past and future mingled, F. Jasmine did not wonder that it was strange and long. So these were the main reasons why F. Jasmine felt, in an unworded way, that this was a morning different from all mornings she had ever known. And of all these facts and feelings the strongest of all was the need to be known for her true self and recognized.

Along the shaded sidewalks on the north side of the town, near the main street, she passed a row of lace-curtained boarding

houses with empty chairs behind the banisters until she came upon a lady sweeping
her front porch. To this lady, after the opening remark about the weather, F. Jasmine
told her plans and, as with the Portuguese in
the Blue Moon Café and all the other
people she was to meet that day, the telling
of the wedding had an end and a beginning,
a shape like a song.

First, just at the moment she commenced,
a sudden hush came in her heart; then, as
the names were named and the plan un-
folded, there was a wild rising lightness and
at the end content. The lady meanwhile
leaned on the broom, listening. Behind her
there was a dark open hall, with a bare
stairway, and to the left a table for letters,
and from this dark hall came the strong hot
smell of cooking turnip greens. The strong
waves of smell and the dark hall seemed to
mingle with F. Jasmine's joy, and when she
looked into the lady's eyes, she loved her,
though she did not even know her name.

The lady neither argued nor accused. She
did not say anything. Until at the very end,
just as F. Jasmine turned to go, she said:
'Well, I declare.' But already F. Jasmine, a
quick gay band tune marching her feet, was
hurrying on her way again.

In a neighbourhood of shaded summer lawns she turned down a side street and met some men mending the road. The sharp smell of melted tar and hot gravel and the loud tractor filled the air with noisy excitement. It was the tractor-man F. Jasmine chose to hear her plans – running beside him, her head thrown back to watch his sunburned face, she had to cup her hands around her mouth to make her voice heard. Even so it was uncertain if he understood, for when she stopped, he laughed and yelled back to her something she could not quite catch. Here, among the racket and excitement, was the place F. Jasmine saw the ghost of the old Frankie plainest of all – hovering close to the commotion, chewing a great big lump of tar, hanging around at noon to watch the lunch-pails being opened. There was a fine big motor-cycle parked near the street-menders, and before going on F. Jasmine looked at it admiringly, then spat on the broad leather seat and shined it carefully with her fist. She was in a very nice neighbourhood near the edge of town, a place of new brick houses with flower-bordered sidewalks and cars parked in paved driveways; but the finer the neighbourhood, the fewer people are about, so F. Jasmine turned back towards the centre of the town. The sun burned like an iron lid on her head and her slip was stuck wet to her chest, and even the organdie dress was wet and clinging in spots also. The march tune had softened to a dreaming song on a violin that slowed her footsteps to a wander. To this kind of music she crossed to the opposite side of the town, beyond the main street and the mill, to the grey crooked streets of the mill section, where, among the choking dust and sad grey rotten shacks, there were more listeners to tell about the wedding.

(From time to time, as she went around, a little conversation buzzed on the bottom of her mind. It was the voice of Berenice when later she would know about this morning. And you just roamed around, the voice said, taking up with total strangers! I never heard of such a thing in all my life! So the Berenice voice sounded, heard but unnoticed like the buzzing of a fly.)

From the sad alleys and crooked streets of the mill section she crossed the unseen line dividing Sugarville from the white people's town. Here were the same two-room shacks and rotted privies, as in the mill section, but round, thick chinaberry trees cast solid shade and often cool ferns grew in pots upon the porches. This was a part of town well known to her, and as she walked along she found herself remembering these familiar lanes in long-past times and other weathers – the ice-pale mornings in the wintertime when even the orange fires under the black iron pots of washwomen seemed to be shivering, the windy autumn nights.

Meanwhile, the glare was dizzy bright and she met and talked to many people, some known to her by sight and name, some strangers. The plans about the wedding stiffened and fixed with each new telling and finally came unchangeable. By eleven-thirty she was very tired, and even the tunes dragged with exhaustion; the need to be recognized for her true self was for the time being satisfied. So she went back to the place from which she started – to the main street where the glittering sidewalks were baked and half-deserted in the white glare.

Always she went by her father's store when-ever she came to town. Her father's store was on the same block as the Blue Moon, but two doors from the main street and in a much better location. It was a narrow store with precious jewels in velvet boxes placed in the window. Beyond the window was her father's workbench, and when you walked along the sidewalk you could see her father working there, his head bent over the tiny watches, and his big brown hands hovered as carefully as butterflies. You could see her father like a public person in the town, well known to all by sight and name. But her father was not proud and did not even look up at those who stopped and gazed at him. This morning, however, he was not at his bench, but behind the counter rolling down his shirtsleeves as though making ready to put on his coat and go outside.

The long glass showcase was bright with jewels and watches and silverware and the store smelled of watch-fixing kerosene. Her father wiped the sweat from his long upper lip with his forefinger and rubbed his nose in a troubled way.

'Where in the world have you been all morning? Berenice has called here twice trying to locate you.'

'I've been all over the whole town,' she said.

But he did not listen. 'I'm going around to your Aunt Pet's,' he said. 'She's had a sad piece of news today.'

'What sad piece of news?' F. Jasmine asked.

'Uncle Charles is dead.'

Uncle Charles was the great-uncle of John Henry West, but though she and John

Henry were first cousins, Uncle Charles was not blood kin to her. He lived twenty-one miles out on the Renfroe Road in a shaded wooden country house surrounded by red cotton fields. An old, old man, he had been sick a long time; it was said he had one foot in the grave – and he always wore bedroom slippers. Now he was dead. But that had nothing to do with the wedding, and so F. Jasmine only said: 'Poor Uncle Charles. That certainy is a pity.'

Her father went back behind the grey sour velvet curtain that divided the store into two parts, the larger public part in front and behind a small dusty private part. Behind the curtain was the water cooler, some shelves of boxes, and the big iron safe where diamond rings were locked away from robbers in the night. F. Jasmine heard her Papa moving around back there, and she settled herself carefully at the work-bench before the front window. A watch, already taken apart, was laid out on the green blotter.

There was a strong streak of watchmaker's blood in her and always the old Frankie had loved to sit at her father's bench. She would put on her father's glasses with the jeweller's loupe attached and, scowling busily, dip them in gasoline. She worked with the lathe, too. Sometimes a little crowd of sidewalk lazies would collect to watch her from the street and she would imagine how they said: 'Frankie Addams works for her father and makes fifteen dollars a week. She fixes the hardest watches in the store and goes to the Woodmen of the World Club with her father. Look at her. She is a credit to the family and a big credit to the whole town.' So she would imagine these conversations, as she scowled with a busy expression at a watch. But now today she looked down at the watch spread out on the blotter, and did not put on the jeweller's loupe. There was something more she ought to say about the death of Uncle Charles.

When her father returned to the front of the store, she said: 'At one time Uncle Charles was one of the leading citizens. It will be a loss to the whole county.'

The words did not seem to impress her father. 'You had better go on home. Berenice has been phoning to locate you.'

'Well, remember you said I could get a wedding dress. And stockings and shoes.'

'Charge them at MacDougal's.'

'I don't see why we always have to trade at MacDougal's just because it's a local store,' she grumbled as she went out of the door.

'Where I am going there will be stores a hundred times bigger than MacDougal's.'

The clock in the tower of the First Baptist Church clanged twelve, the mill whistle wailed. There was a drowsing quietness about the street, and even the very cars, parked slantwise with their noses towards the centre aisle of grass, were like exhausted cars that have all gone to sleep. The few people out at the noon hour kept close beneath the blunt shade of the awnings. The sun took the colour from the sky and the brick stores seemed shrunken, dark, beneath the glare – one building had an overhanging cornice at the top which, from a distance, gave it the queer look of a brick building that has begun to melt. In this noon quietness, she heard again the organ of the monkey-man, the sound that always magnetized her footsteps so that she automatically went towards it. This time she would find them and tell them good-bye.

As F. Jasmine hurried down the street, she saw the two of them in her mind's eye – and wondered if they would remember her. The old Frankie had always loved the monkey and the monkey-man. They resembled each other – they both had an anxious, question-ing expression, as though they wondered every minute if what they did was wrong. The monkey, in fact, was nearly always wrong; after he danced to the organ tune, he was supposed to take off his darling little cap and pass it around to the audience, but likely as not he would get mixed up and bow and reach out his cap to the monkey-man, and not the audience. And the monkey-man would plead with him, and finally begin to chatter and fuss. When he would make as if to slap the monkey, the monkey would cringe down and chatter also – and they would look at each other with the same scared exasperation, their wrinkled faces very sad. After watching them a long time, the old Frankie, fascinated, began to take on the same expression as she followed them around. And now F. Jasmine was eager to see them.

She could hear the broken-sounding organ plainly, although they were not on the main street, but up farther and probably just around the corner of the next block. So F. Jasmine hurried towards them. As she neared the corner, she heard other sounds that puzzled her curiosity so that she listened and stopped. Above the music of the organ there was the sound of a man's voice quarrelling and the excited higher fussing of the monkey-man. She could hear the monkey chattering also. Then suddenly the organ stopped and the two different voices were loud and mad. F. Jasmine had reached the corner, and it was the corner by the Sears and Roebuck store; she passed the store slowly, then turned and faced a curious sight.

It was a narrow street that went downhill towards Front Avenue, blinding bright in the wild glare. There on the sidewalk was the monkey, the monkey-man, and a soldier holding out a whole fistful of dollar bills – it looked at the first glance like a hundred dollars. The soldier looked angry, and the monkey-man was pale and excited also. Their voices were quarrelling and F. Jasmine gathered that the soldier was trying to buy the monkey. The monkey himself was crouched and shivering down on the sidewalk close to the brick wall of the Sears and Roebuck store. In spite of the hot day, he had on his little red coat with silver buttons and his little face, scared and desperate, had the look of someone who is just about to sneeze. Shivering and pitiful, he kept bowing at nobody and offering his cap into the air. He knew the furious voices were about him and he felt blamed.

F. Jasmine was standing nearby, trying to take in the commotion, listening and still.

Then suddenly the soldier grabbed at the monkey's chain, but the monkey screamed, and before she knew what it was all about, the monkey had skittered up her leg and body and was huddled on her shoulder with his little monkey hands around her head. It happened in a flash, and she was so shocked she could not move. The voices stopped and, except for the monkey's jibbered scream, the street was silent. The soldier stood slack-jawed, surprised, still holding out the handful of dollar bills.

The monkey-man was the first to recover; he spoke to the monkey in a gentle voice, and in another second the monkey sprang from off her shoulder and landed on the organ which the monkey-man was carrying on his back. The two of them went away. They quickly hurried around the corner and at the last second, just as they turned, they both looked back with the same expression – reproaching and sly. F. Jasmine leaned against the brick wall, and she still felt the monkey on her shoulder and smelt his dusty, sour smell; she shivered. The soldier muttered until the pair of them were out of sight, and F. Jasmine noticed then that he was red-haired and the same soldier who had been in the Blue Moon. He stuffed the bills in his side pocket.

'He certainly is a darling monkey,' F. Jasmine said. 'But it gave me a mighty funny feeling to have him run up me like that.'

The soldier seemed to realize her for the first time. The look on his face changed slowly, and the angry expression went away. He was looking at F. Jasmine from the top of her head, down the organdie best dress, and to the black pumps she was wearing.

'I guess you must have wanted the monkey a whole lot,' she said. 'I've always wanted a monkey, too.'

'What?' he asked. Then he remarked in a muffled voice, as if his tongue were made of felt or a very thick piece of blotting paper, 'Which way are we going? Are you going my way or am I going yours?'

F. Jasmine had not expected this. The soldier was joining with her like a traveller who meets another traveller in a tourist town. For a second, it occurred to her that she had heard this remark before, perhaps in a picture show – that furthermore it was a set remark requiring a set answer. Not knowing the ready-made reply, she answered carefully.

'Which way are you going?'

'Hook on,' he said, sticking out his elbow. They walked down the side street, on their shrunken noontime shadows. The soldier was the only person during that day who spoke first to F. Jasmine and invited her to join with him. But, when she began to tell about the wedding, something seemed lacking. Perhaps it was because she had already told her plans to so many people all over town that now she could rest satisfied. Or perhaps it was because she felt the soldier was not really listening. He looked at the pink organdie dress from the corner of his eye, and there was a half-smile on his mouth. F. Jasmine could not match her steps to his, although she tried, for his legs seemed loosely fastened to his body so that he walked in a rambling way.

'What state do you come from, if I may ask?' she said politely.

In the second that passed before his answer there was time for her skimming mind to picture Hollywood, New York, and Maine. The soldier answered: 'Arkansas.'

Now of all the forty-eight states in the Union, Arkansas was one of the very few that had never especially appealed to her – but her imagination, balked, immediately turned the opposite way so that she asked:

'Do you have any idea where you will be going?'

'Just banging around,' the soldier said.

'I'm out loose on a three day pass.'

He had mistaken the meaning of her question, for she had asked it to him as a soldier liable to be sent to any foreign country in the world, but, before she could explain what she had meant, he said:

'There's a kind of hotel around the corner I'm staying at.' Then, still looking at the pleated collar of her dress, he added: 'It seems like I've seen you somewhere before. Do you ever go dancing at the Idle Hour?'

They walked down Front Avenue, and now the street was beginning to have the air of Saturday afternoon. A lady was drying her yellow hair in the window of the second floor above the fish store, and she called down to two soldiers who passed along the street. A street preacher, a known town character, was preaching on a corner to a group of warehouse coloured boys and scraggly children. But F. Jasmine did not have her mind on what was going on around her. The soldier's mention of dancing and the Idle Hour touched like a story-tale wand upon her mind. She realized for the first time that she was walking with a soldier, with one of the groups of loud, glad gangs that roamed around the streets together or walked with the grown girls. They danced at the Idle

Hour and had a good time, while the old Frankie was asleep. And she had never danced with anybody, excepting Evelyn Owen, and had never put foot in the Idle Hour.

And now F. Jasmine walked with a soldier who in his mind included her in such unknown pleasures. But she was not altogether proud. There was an uneasy doubt that she could not quite place or name. The noon air was thick and sticky as hot syrup, and there was the stifling smell of the dye-rooms from the cotton mill. She heard the organ-grinder sounding faintly from the main street.

The soldier stopped: 'This is the hotel,' he said.

They were before the Blue Moon and F. Jasmine was surprised to hear it spoken of as a hotel, as she had thought it was only a café. When the soldier held the screen door open for her, she noticed that he swayed a little. Her eyes saw blinding red, then black, after the glare, and it took them a minute to get used to the blue light. She followed the soldier to one of the booths on the right.

'Care for a beer,' he said, not in an asking voice, but as though he took her reply for granted.

F. Jasmine did not enjoy the taste of beer; once or twice she had sneaked swallows from her father's glass and it was sour. But the soldier had not left her any choice. 'I would be delighted,' she said. 'Thank you.'

Never had she been in a hotel, although she had often thought about them and written about them in her shows. Her father had stayed in hotels several times, and once, from Montgomery, he had brought her two little tiny cakes of hotel soap which she had saved. She looked around the Blue Moon with new curiosity. All of a sudden she felt very proper. On seating herself at the booth table, she carefully smoothed down her dress, as she did when at a party or in church, so as not to sit the pleats out of the skirt. She sat up straight and on her face there was a proper expression. But the Blue Moon still seemed to her more like a kind of café than a real hotel. She did not see the sad, pale Portuguese, and a laughing fat lady with a golden tooth poured beer for the soldier at the counter. The stairway at the back led probably to the hotel rooms upstairs, and the steps were lighted by a blue neon bulb and covered with a runner of linoleum. A sassy chorus on the radio was singing an advertisement: Denteen Chewing Gum!

Denteen Chewing Gum! Denteen! The beery air reminded her of a room where a rat has died behind a wall. The soldier walked back to the booth, carrying two glasses of the beer; he licked some foam that had spilled over his hand and wiped the hand on his trousers seat. When he was settled in the booth, F. Jasmine said, in a voice that was absolutely new to her – a high voice spoken through the nose, dainty and dignified:

'Don't you think it is mighty exciting? Here we are sitting here at this table and in a month from now there's no telling where on earth we'll be. Maybe tomorrow the army will send you to Alaska like they sent my brother. Or to France or Africa or Burma. And I don't have any idea where I will be. I'd like for us to go to Alaska for a while, and then go somewhere else. They say that Paris has been liberated. In my opinion the war will be over next month.'

The soldier raised his glass, and threw back his head to gulp the beer. F. Jasmine took a few swallows also, although it tasted nasty to her. Today she did not see the world as loose and cracked and turning a thousand miles an hour, so that the spinning views of war and distant lands made her mind dizzy. The world had never been so close to her. Sitting across from the soldier at that booth in the Blue Moon, she suddenly saw the three of them – herself, her brother, and the bride – walking beneath a cold Alaskan sky, along the sea where green ice waves lay frozen and folded on the shore; they climbed a sunny glacier shot through with pale cold colours and a rope tied the three of them together, and friends from another glacier called in Alaskan their J A names. She saw them next in Africa, where, with a crowd of sheeted Arabs, they galloped on camels in the sandy wind. Burma was jungle-dark, and she had seen pictures in *Life* magazine. Because of the wedding, these distant lands, the world, seemed altogether possible and near: as close to Winter Hill as Winter Hill was to the town. It was the actual present, in fact, that seemed to F. Jasmine a little bit unreal.

'Yes, it's mighty exciting,' she said again.

The soldier, his beer finished, wiped his wet mouth with the back of his freckled hand. His face, although not fat, seemed swollen, and it was glossy in the neon light. He had a thousand little freckles, and the only thing that seemed to her pretty was his bright, red curly hair. His eyes were blue, set close together, and the whites were raw. He was staring at her with a peculiar expression, not as one traveller gazes at another, but as a person who shares a secret scheme. For several minutes he did not talk. Then, when at last he spoke, the words did not make sense to her and she did not understand. It seemed to her the soldier said:

'Who is a cute dish?'

There were no dishes on the table and she had the uneasy feeling he had begun to talk a kind of double-talk. She tried to turn the conversation.

'I told you my brother is a Member of the Armed Forces.'

But the soldier did not seem to listen. 'I could of sworn I'd run into you some place before.'

The doubt in F. Jasmine deepened. She realized now that the soldier thought she was much older than she was, but her pleasure in this was somehow uncertain. To make conversation she remarked:

'Some people are not partial to red hair. But to me it's my favourite colour.' She added, remembering her brother and the bride. 'Except dark brown and yellow. I always think it's a pity for the Lord to waste curly hair on boys. When so many girls are going around with hair as straight as pokers.'

The soldier leaned over the booth table

and, still staring at her, he began to walk his fingers, the second and third fingers of both hands, across the table towards her. The fingers were dirty, with rinds of black beneath the nails. F. Jasmine had the sense that something strange was going to happen, when just at that moment there was a sudden racket and commotion and three or four soldiers shoved each other into the hotel. There was a babble of voices and the screen door banged. The soldier's fingers stopped walking across the table and, when he glanced at the other soldiers, the peculiar expression was scattered from his eyes.

'That certainy is a darling little monkey,' she said.

'What monkey?'

The doubt deepened to the feeling that something was wrong. 'Why, the monkey you tried to buy a few minutes ago. What's the matter with you?'

Something was wrong and the soldier put his fists up to his head. His body limpened and he leaned back in the seat of the booth, as though collapsed. 'Oh, that monkey!' he said in his slurred voice. 'The walk in the sun after all those beers. I was slamming around all night.' He sighed, and his hands were open loose upon the table. 'I guess maybe I'm just about beat.'

For the first time F. Jasmine began to wonder what she was doing there and if she ought not to take herself on home. The other soldiers had crowded around a table near the stairway, and the lady with the golden tooth was busy behind the counter. F. Jasmine had finished her beer and a lace of creamy foam lined the inside of the empty glass. The hot, close smell in the hotel suddenly made her feel a little queer.

'I have to go home now. Thank you for treating me.'

She got up from the booth, but the soldier reached out towards her and caught a piece of her dress. 'Hey!' he said. 'Don't just walk off like that. Let's fix up something for this evening. How bout a date for nine o'clock?'

'A date?' F. Jasmine felt as though her head was big and loose. The beer made her legs feel peculiar, too, almost as though she had four legs to manage instead of two. On any other day than this it would have seemed almost impossible that anyone, much less a soldier, would have invited her to a date. The very word, *date,* was a grown word used by older girls. But here again there was a blight upon her pleasure. If he knew she was not yet thirteen, he would never have invited her, or probably never joined with her at all. There was a troubled sense, a light uneasiness. 'I don't know–'

'Sure,' he urged. 'Suppose we link up here at nine o'clock. We can go to the Idle Hour or something. That suit you all right? Here at nine o'clock.'

'O.K.' she said finally. 'I will be delighted.

Again she was on the burning sidewalk, where passing walkers looked dark and shrunken in the angry glare. It took her a while to come back to the wedding feeling of that morning, for the half-hour in the hotel had slightly distracted her frame of mind. But it did not take her very long, and by the time she reached the main street, the wedding feeling was recovered. She met a little girl, two grades below her at the school, and stopped her on the street to tell her her plans. She told her also that a soldier had invited her to have a date, and now she told it in a bragging tone. The girl went with her to buy the wedding clothes, which took an hour and meant the trying-on of more than a dozen beautiful dresses.

But the main thing that brought back the wedding frame of mind was an accident that occurred on the way home. It was a mysterious trick of sight and the imagination.

She was walking home when all at once there was a shock in her as though a thrown knife struck and shivered in her chest. F. Jasmine stopped dead in her tracks, one foot still raised, and at first she could not take in just what had happened. There was something sideways and behind her that had flashed across the very corner edge of her left eye; she had half-seen something, a dark double shape, in the alley she had just that moment passed. And because of this half-seen object, the quick flash in the corner of her eye, there had sprung up in her the sudden picture of her brother and the bride. Ragged and bright as lightning she saw the two of them as they had been when, for a moment, they stood together before the living-room mantelpiece, his arm around her shoulders. So strong was this picture that F. Jasmine felt suddenly that Jarvis and Janice were there behind her in the alley, and she had caught a glimpse of them – although she knew, and well enough, that they were in Winter Hill, almost a hundred miles away.

F. Jasmine lowered her raised foot to the pavement and slowly turned to look around. The alley lay between two grocery stores: a narrow alley, dark in the glare. She did not look at it directly, for somehow it was as though she was almost afraid. Her eyes stole slowly down the brick wall and she glimpsed again the dark double shadow. And what was there? F. Jasmine was stunned. There in the alley were only two coloured boys, one taller than the other and with his arm resting on the shorter boy's shoulder. That was all – but something about the angle or the way they stood, or the pose of their shapes, had reflected the sudden picture of her brother and the bride that had so shocked her. And with this vision of them plain and exact the morning ended, and she was home by two o'clock.

2

The afternoon was like the centre of the cake that Berenice had baked last Monday, a cake which failed. The old Frankie had been glad the cake had failed, not out of spite, but because she loved these fallen cakes the best. She enjoyed the damp, gummy richness near the centre, and did not understand why grown people thought such cakes a failure. It was a loaf cake, that last Monday, with the edge risen light and high and the middle moist and altogether fallen – after the bright, high morning the afternoon was dense and solid as the centre of that cake. And because it was the last of all the afternoons, F. Jasmine found an unfamiliar sweetness in the known old kitchen ways and tones. At two o'clock, when she came in, Berenice was pressing clothes. John Henry sat at the table blowing soap-bubbles with a spool, and he gave her a long, green, secret look.

'Where in the world have you been?' asked Berenice.

'We know something you don't know,' John Henry said. 'Do you know what?'

'What?'

'Berenice and me are going to the wedding.'

F. Jasmine was taking off her organdie dress, and his words startled her.

'Uncle Charles is dead.'

'I heard that, but–'

'Yes,' said Berenice. 'The poor old soul passed on this morning. They're taking the body to the family graveyard in Opelika. And John Henry is to stay with us for several days.'

Now that she knew the death of Uncle Charles would in a sense affect the wedding, she made room for it in her thoughts. While Berenice finished pressing clothes, F. Jasmine sat in her petticoat on the stairs leading up to her room; she closed her eyes. Uncle Charles lived in a shady wooden house out in the country, and he was too old to eat corn on the cob. In June of this summer he took sick, and ever since he had been critical. He lay in the bed, shrunken and brown and very old. He complained that the pictures were hung crooked on the wall, and they took down all the framed pictures – it was not that. He complained that his bed was placed in a wrong corner, and so they moved his bed – it was not that. Then his voice failed, and when he tried to talk, it was as though his throat had filled with glue, and they could not understand the words. One Sunday the Wests had gone out to see him and taken Frankie with them; she had tiptoed to the open door of the back bedroom. He looked like an old man carved in brown wood and covered with a sheet. Only his eyes had moved, and they were like blue jelly, and she had felt they might come out from the sockets and roll like blue wet jelly down his stiff face. She had stood in the doorway staring at him – then tiptoed away, afraid. They finally made out that he complained the sun shone the wrong way through the window, but that was not the thing that hurt him so. And it was death.

F. Jasmine opened her eyes and stretched herself.

'It is a terrible thing to be dead!' she said.

'Well,' said Berenice. 'The old man suffered a lot and he had lived up his span. The Lord appointed the time for him.'

'I know. But at the same time it seems mighty queer that he would have to die the very day before the wedding. And why on earth do you and John Henry have to go tagging to the wedding? Seems to me like you would just stay home.'

'Frankie Addams,' said Berenice, and she suddenly put her arms akimbo, 'you are the most selfish human being that ever breathed. We all been cooped up in this kitchen and–'

'Don't call me Frankie!' she said. 'I don't wish to have to remind you any more.'

It was the time of early afternoon when in the old days a sweet band would be playing. Now with the radio turned off, the kitchen was solemn and silent and there were sounds from far away. A coloured voice called from the sidewalk, calling the names of vegetables in a dark slurred tone, a long unwinding hollering in which there were no words. Somewhere, near in the neighbourhood, there was the sound of a hammer and each stroke left a round echo.

'You would be mighty surprised if you knew whereall I've been today. I was all over this whole town. I saw the monkey and the monkey-man. There was this soldier who was trying to buy the monkey and holding a hundred dollars in his hand. Have you ever seen anybody try to buy a monkey on the street?'

'No. Was he drunk?'

'Drunk?' F. Jasmine said.

'Oh,' said John Henry. 'The monkey and the monkey-man!'

Berenice's question had disturbed F. Jasmine, and she took a minute to consider. 'I don't think he was drunk. People don't get drunk in broad daylight.' She had meant to tell Berenice about the soldier, but now she hesitated. 'All the same there was something–' Her voice trailed at the end, and she watched a rainbow soap-bubble floating in silence across the room. Here in the kitchen, barefooted and wearing only her petticoat, it was hard to realize and judge the soldier. About the promise for that evening she felt double-minded. The indecision bothered her, and so she changed the subject. 'I hope you washed and ironed everything good of mine today. I have to take them to Winter Hill.'

'What for?' said Berenice. 'You only going to be there just one day.'

'You heard me,' F. Jasmine said. 'I told you I wasn't coming back here after the wedding.'

'Fool's hill. You have a whole lot less of sense than I was giving you credit for. What makes you think they want to take you along with them? Two is company and three is a crowd. And that is the main thing about a wedding. Two is company and three is a crowd.'

F. Jasmine always found it hard to argue with a known saying. She loved to use them in her shows and in her conversation, but they were very hard to argue with, and so she said:

'You wait and see.'

'Remember back to the time of the flood? Remember Noah and the ark?'

'And what has that got to do with it?' she asked.

'Remember the way he admitted them creatures.'

'Oh, hush up your big old mouth,' she said.

'Two by two,' said Berenice. 'He admitted them creatures two by two.'

The argument that afternoon was, from the

beginning to the end, about the wedding. Berenice refused to follow F. Jasmine's frame of mind. From the first it was as though she tried to catch F. Jasmine by the collar, like the Law catches a no-good in the wrong, and jerk her back where she had started – back to the sad and crazy summer that now seemed to F. Jasmine like a time remembered from long ago. But F. Jasmine was stubborn and not to be caught. Berenice had flaws to find in all of her ideas, and from the first word to the last she did her terrible, level best to try to deny the wedding. But F. Jasmine would not let it be denied.

'Look,' F. Jasmine said, and she picked up the pink organdie dress that she had just taken off. 'Remember when I bought this dress the collar had teeny little pleats. But you have been ironing the collar like it was supposed to be ruffled. Now we got to set those little pleats like they ought to be.'

'And who is going to do it?' said Berenice. She picked up the dress and judged the collar. 'I got more to do with my time and trouble.'

'Well, it's got to be done,' F. Jasmine argued. 'It's the way the collar is supposed to be. And besides, I might be wearing it out somewhere this evening.'

'And where, pray tell me?' said Berenice. 'Answer the question I asked when you came in. Where in the world have you been all morning?'

It was exactly as F. Jasmine had known it would be – the way Berenice refused to understand. And, since it was more a matter of feelings than of words or facts, she found it difficult to explain. When she spoke of connexions, Berenice gave her a long, uncomprehending stare – and, when she went on to the Blue Moon and the many people, the broad, flat nose of Berenice widened and she shook her head. F. Jasmine did not mention the soldier; although she was on the verge of speaking of him several times, something warned her not to.

When she had finished, Berenice said:

'Frankie, I honestly believe you have turned crazy on us. Walking around all over town and telling total strangers this big tale. You know in your soul this mania of yours is pure foolishness.'

'You wait and see,' F. Jasmine said. 'They will take me.'

'And if they don't?'

F. Jasmine picked up the shoe box with the silver slippers and the wrapped box with the wedding dress. 'These are my wedding clothes. I'll show them to you later.'

'And if they don't?'

F. Jasmine had already started up the stairs, but she stopped and turned back towards the kitchen. The room was silent.

'If they don't, I will kill myself,' she said. 'But they will.'

'Kill yourself how?' asked Berenice.

'I will shoot myself in the side of the head with a pistol.'

'Which pistol?'

'The pistol that Papa keeps under his handkerchiefs along with Mother's picture in the right-hand bureau drawer.'

Berenice did not answer for a minute and her face was a puzzle. 'You heard what Mr Addams told you about playing with that pistol. Go on upstairs now. Dinner will be ready in a little while.'

It was a late dinner, this last meal that the three of them would ever eat together at the kitchen table. On Saturdays they were not regular about the times of meals, and they began the dinner at four o'clock, when already the August sun was slanting long and stale across the yard. It was the time of afternoon when the bars of sunlight crossed the back yard like the bars of a bright strange jail. The two fig trees were green and flat, the arbour sun-crossed and casting solid shade. The sun in the afternoon did not slant through the back window of the house, so that the kitchen was grey. The three of them began their dinner at four o'clock, and the dinner lasted until twilight. There was hopping-john cooked with the ham bone, and as they ate they began to talk of love. It was a subject F. Jasmine had never talked about in all her life. In the first place, she had never believed in love and had never put any of it in her shows. But this afternoon when Berenice began this conversation, F. Jasmine did not stop up both her ears, but as she quietly ate the peas and rice and pot-liquor she listened.

'I have heard of many a queer thing,' said Berenice. 'I have knew mens to fall in love with girls so ugly that you wonder if their eyes is straight. I have seen some of the most peculiar weddings anybody could con-jecture. Once I knew a boy with his whole faced burned off so that–'

'Who?' asked John Henry.

Berenice swallowed a piece of cornbread and wiped her mouth with the back of her hand. 'I have knew womens to love veritable Satans and thank Jesus when they put their split hooves over the threshold. I have knew boys to take it into their heads to fall in love with other boys. You know Lily Mae Jenkins?'

F. Jasmine thought a minute, and then answered: 'I'm not sure.'

'Well, you either know him or you don't know him. He prisses around with a pink satin blouse and one arm akimbo. Now this Lily Mae fell in love with a man name Juney Jones. A man, mind you. And Lily Mae turned into a girl. He changed his nature and his sex and turned into a girl.'

'Honest?' F. Jasmine asked. 'Did he really?'

'He did,' said Berenice. 'To all intents and purposes.'

F. Jasmine scratched behind her ear and said: 'It's funny I can't think who you are talking about. I used to think I knew so many people.'

'Well, you don't need to know Lily Mae Jenkins. You can live without knowing him.'

'Anyway, I don't believe you,' F. Jasmine said.

'Well, I ain't arguing with you,' said Berenice. 'What was it we was speaking about?'

'About peculiar things.'

'Oh, yes.'

They stopped off a few minutes to get on with the dinner. F. Jasmine ate with her elbows on the table and her bare heels hooked on the rungs of the chair. She and Berenice sat opposite each other, and John Henry faced the window. Now hopping-john was F. Jasmine's very favourite food. She had always warned them to wave a plate of rice and peas before her nose when she was in her coffin, to make certain there was no mistake; for if a breath of life was left in her, she would sit up and eat, but if she smelled the hopping-john and did not stir, then they could just nail down the coffin and be certain that she was truly dead. Now Berenice had chosen for her death-test a piece of fried fresh-water trout, and for John Henry it was divinity fudge. But though F. Jasmine loved the hopping-john the very best, the others also liked it well enough, and all three of them enjoyed the dinner that day: the ham knuckle, the hopping-john, cornbread, hot baked sweet potatoes, and the buttermilk. And as they ate, they carried on the conversation.

'Yes, as I was just now telling you,' said Berenice, 'I have seen many peculiar things in my day. But one thing I never knew and never heard tell about. No siree, I never did.'

Berenice stopped talking and sat there shaking her head, waiting for them to question her. But F. Jasmine would not speak.

And it was John Henry who raised his curious face from his plate and asked: 'What, Berenice?'

'No,' said Berenice. 'I never before in all my days heard of anybody falling in love with a wedding. I have knew many peculiar things, but I never heard of that before.'

F. Jasmine grumbled something.

'So I have been thinking it over and have come to a conclusion.'

'How?' John Henry suddenly asked. 'How did that boy change into a girl?'

Berenice glanced at him and straightened the napkin tied around his neck. 'It was just one of them things, Candy Lamb. I don't know.'

'Don't listen at her,' F. Jasmine said.

'So I have been thinking it over in my mind and come to this conclusion. What you ought to begin thinking about is a beau.'

'What?' F. Jasmine asked.

'You heard me,' said Berenice. 'A beau. A nice little white boy beau.'

F. Jasmine put down her fork and sat with her head turned to one side. 'I don't want any beau. What would I do with one?'

'Do, Foolish?' asked Berenice. 'Why, make him treat you to the picture show. For one thing.'

F. Jasmine pulled the bangs of her hair down over her forehead and slid her feet across the rung of the chair.

'Now you belong to change from being so rough and greedy and big,' said Berenice. 'You ought to fix yourself up nice in your dresses. And speak sweetly and act sly.'

F. Jasmine said in a low voice: 'I'm not rough and greedy any more. I already changed that way.'

'Well, excellent,' said Berenice. 'Now catch you a beau.'

F. Jasmine wanted to tell Berenice about the soldier, the hotel, and the invitation for the evening date. But something checked her, and she hinted around the edges of the subject: 'What kind of a beau? Do you mean something like–' F. Jasmine paused, for at home in the kitchen that last afternoon, the soldier seemed unreal.

'Now that I cannot advise,' said Berenice. 'You got to decide for yourself.'

'Something like a soldier who would may-be take me dancing at the Idle Hour?' She did not look at Berenice.

'Who is talking about soldiers and dancing? I'm talking about a nice little white boy beau your own age. How about that little old Barney?'

'Barney MacKean?'

'Why, certainy. He would do very well to begin with. You could make out with him until somebody else comes along. He would do.'

'That mean nasty Barney!' The garage had been dark, with thin needling sunlight coming through the cracks of the closed door, and with the smell of dust. But she did not let herself remember the unknown sin that he had showed her, that later made her want to throw a knife between his eyes. Instead, she shook herself hard and began mashing peas and rice together on her plate. 'You are the biggest crazy in this town.'

'The crazy calls the sane the crazy.'

So they began to eat again, all except John Henry. F. Jasmine was busy slicing open cornbread and spreading it with butter and mashing her hopping-john and drinking milk. Berenice ate more slowly, peeling off bits of ham from the knuckle in a dainty way. John Henry looked from one of them to the other, and after listening to their talk he had stopped eating to think for a little while. Then after a minute he asked:

'How many of them did you catch? Them beaus.'

'How many?' said Berenice. 'Lamb, how

many hairs is in these plaits? You talking to Berenice Sadie Brown.'

So Berenice was started and her voice went on and on. And when she had begun this way, on a long and serious subject, the words flowed one into the other and her voice began to sing. In the grey of the kitchen on summer afternoons the tone of her voice was golden and quiet, and you could listen to the colour and the singing of her voice and not follow the words. F. Jasmine let the long tones linger and spin inside her ears, but her mind did not stamp the voice with sense or sentences. She sat there listening at the table, and now and then she thought of a fact that all her life had seemed to her most curious: Berenice always spoke of herself as though she was somebody very beautiful. Almost on this one subject, Berenice was really not in her right mind. F. Jasmine listened to the voice and stared at Berenice across the table: the dark face with the wild blue eye, the eleven greased plaits that fitted her head like a skull-cap, the wide flat nose that quivered as she spoke. And whatever else Berenice might be, she was not beautiful. It seemed to her she ought to give Berenice advice. So she said at the next pause:

'I think you ought to quit worrying about beaus and be content with T.T. I bet you are forty years old. It is time for you to settle down.'

Berenice bunched up her lips and stared at F. Jasmine with the dark live eye. 'Wisemouth,' she said. 'How do you know so much? I got as much right as anybody else to continue to have a good time so long as I can. And as far as that goes, I'm not so old as some people would try and make out. I can still ministrate. And I got many a long year ahead of me before I resign myself to a corner.'

'Well, I didn't mean go into a corner,' F. Jasmine said.

'I heard what you meant,' said Berenice.

John Henry had been watching and listening, and there was a little crust of pot-liquor around his mouth. A big blue lazy fly was hovering around him and trying to light on his sticky face, so that from time to time John Henry waved his hand to shoo the fly away.

'Did they all treat you to the picture show?' he asked. 'All those beaus.'

'To the show, or to one thing or another,' she answered.

'You mean you never pay your own way?' John Henry asked.

'That's what I'm telling you,' said Berenice. 'Not when I go out with a beau. Now if I was to go somewhere with a crowd of womens, I would have to pay my way. But I'm not the kind of person to go around with crowds of womens.'

'When you all took the trip to Fairview—' F. Jasmine said – for one Sunday that last spring there had been a coloured pilot who took up coloured people in his aeroplane. 'Who paid the way?'

'Now let me see,' said Berenice. 'Honey and Clorina took care of their expense, except I loaned Honey one dollar and forty cents. Cape Clyde paid his own way. And T.T. paid for himself and for me.'

'Then T.T. treated you to the aeroplane ride?'

'That's what I'm telling you. He paid the bus tickets to and from Fairview and the aeroplane ride and the refreshments. The complete trip. Why, naturally he paid the way. How else do you think I could afford to fly around in an aeroplane? Me making six dollars a week.'

'I didn't realize that,' F. Jasmine admitted finally. 'I wonder where T.T. got all of his money.'

'Earned it,' said Berenice. 'John Henry,

wipe off your mouth.'

So they rested at the table, for the way they ate their meals, this summer, was in rounds: they would eat awhile and then let the food have a chance to spread out and settle inside their stomachs, and a little later they would start in again. F. Jasmine crossed her knife and fork on her empty plate, and began to question Berenice about a matter that had bothered her.

'Tell me. Is it just us who call this hopping-john? Or is it known by that name through all the country? It seems a strange name somehow.'

'Well, I have heard it called various things,' said Berenice.

'What?'

'Well, I have heard it called peas and rice. Or rice and peas and pot-liquor. Or hopping-john. You can vary and take your pick.'

'But I'm not talking about this town,' F. Jasmine said. 'I mean in other places. I mean through all the world. I wonder what the French call it.'

'Oh,' said Berenice. 'Well, you ask me a question I cannot answer.'

'Merci a la parlez,' F. Jasmine said.

They sat at the table and did not speak. F. Jasmine was tilted back in her chair, her head turned towards the window and the sun-crossed empty yard. The town was silent and the kitchen was silent except for the clock. F. Jasmine could not feel the world go round, and nothing moved.

'Now a funny thing has happened to me,' F. Jasmine began. 'I don't hardly know how to tell just what I mean. It was one of those strange things you can't exactly explain.'

'What, Frankie?' John Henry asked.

F. Jasmine turned from the window, but before she could speak again there was the sound. In the silence of the kitchen they heard the tone shaft quietly across the room, then again the same note was repeated. A piano scale slanted across the August afternoon. A chord was struck. Then in a dreaming way a chain of chords climbed slowly upward like a flight of castle stairs: but just at the end, when the eighth chord should have sounded and the scale made complete, there was a stop. This next to the last chord was repeated. The seventh chord, which seems to echo all of the unfinished scale, struck and insisted again and again. And finally there was a silence. F. Jasmine and John Henry and Berenice looked at each other. Somewhere in the neighbourhood an August piano was being tuned.

'Jesus!' said Berenice. 'I seriously believe this will be the last straw.'

John Henry shivered. 'Me too,' he said.

F. Jasmine sat perfectly still before the table crowded with plates and dinner dishes. The grey of the kitchen was a stale grey and the room was too flat and too square. After the silence another note was sounded, and then repeated an octave higher. F. Jasmine raised her eyes each time the tone climbed higher, as though she watched the note move from one part of the kitchen to another; at the highest point her eyes had reached a ceiling corner, then, when a long scale slid downward, her head turned slowly as her eyes crossed from the ceiling corner to the floor corner at the opposite side of the room. The bottom bass note was struck six times, and F. Jasmine was left staring at an old pair of bedroom slippers and an empty beer bottle which were in that corner of the room. Finally she shut her eyes, and shook herself, and got up from the table.

'It makes me sad,' F. Jasmine said. 'And jittery too.' She began to walk around the room. 'They tell me that when they want to punish them over in Milledgeville, they tie them up and make them listen to piano-tuning.' She walked three times around the table. 'There's something I want to ask you. Suppose you ran into somebody who seemed to you terribly peculiar, but you didn't know the reason why.'

'In what ways peculiar?'

F. Jasmine thought of the soldier, but she could not further explain. 'Say you might meet somebody you think he almost might be a *drunk*, but you're not sure about anything. And he wanted you to join with him and go to a big party or dance. What would you do?'

'Well, on the face of it, I don't know. It would depend on how I feel. I might go with him to the big party and meet up with somebody that suited me better.' The live eye of Berenice suddenly narrowed, and she looked hard at F. Jasmine. 'But why do you ask that?'

The quietness in the room stretched out until F. Jasmine could hear the drip-drop from the faucet of the sink. She was trying to frame a way to tell Berenice about the soldier. Then all at once the telephone rang. F. Jasmine jumped up and, turning over her empty milk glass, dashed to the hall – but John Henry, who was nearer, reached the telephone first. He knelt on the telephone chair and smiled into the mouthpiece before he said hello. Then he kept on saying hello until F. Jasmine took the receiver from him and repeated the hellos at least two dozen times before she finally hung up.

'Anything like that makes me so mad,' she said when they had gone back to the kitchen. 'Or when the express truck stops before the door and the man peers at our number and then takes the box somewhere else. I look on those things as a kind of sign.' She raked her fingers through her crew-cut blond hair. 'You know I'm really going to get my fortune told before I leave home in the morning. It's something I've been meaning to do for a long time.'

Berenice said: 'Changing the subject, when are you going to show me the new dress? I'm anxious to see what you selected.'

So F. Jasmine went up to get the dress. Her room was what was known as a hotbox; the heat from the rest of the house rose up to her room and stayed there. In the afternoon the air seemed to make a buzzing sound, so it was a good idea to keep the motor running. F. Jasmine turned on the motor and opened the closet door. Until this day before the wedding she had always kept her six costumes hung in a row on coat-hangers, and she just threw her ordinary clothes up on the shelf or kicked them into a corner. But when she had come home this afternoon, she had changed this: the costumes were thrown up on the shelf and the wedding dress hung alone in the closet on a coat-hanger. The silver slippers were placed carefully on the floor beneath the dress with the toes pointed north, towards Winter Hill. For some reason F. Jasmine tip-toed around the room as she began to dress.

'Shut your eyes!' she called. 'Don't watch me coming down the stairs. Don't open your eyes until I tell you.'

It was as though the four walls of the kitchen watched her, and the skillet hanging on the wall was a watching round black eye. The piano-tuning was for a minute silent. Berenice sat with her head bowed, as though she was in church. And John Henry had his head bowed also, but he was peeking. F. Jasmine stood at the foot of the stairs and placed her left hand on her hip.

'Oh, how pretty!' John Henry said.

Berenice raised her head, and when she saw F. Jasmine her face was a study. The dark eye looked from the silver hair ribbon to the soles of the silver slippers. She said nothing.

'Now tell me your honest opinion,' F. Jasmine said.

148

But Berenice looked at the orange satin evening dress and shook her head and did not comment. At first she shook her head with short little turns, but the longer she stared, the longer these shakes became, until at the last shake F. Jasmine heard her neck crack.

'What's the matter?' F. Jasmine asked.

'I thought you was going to get a pink dress.'

'But when I got in the store I changed my mind. What is wrong with this dress? Don't you like it, Berenice?'

'No,' said Berenice. 'It don't do.'

'What do you mean? It don't do.'

F. Jasmine turned to look in the mirror, and she still thought the dress was beautiful. But Berenice had a sour and stubborn look on her face, an expression like that of an old long-eared mule, and F. Jasmine could not understand.

'But I don't see what you mean,' she complained. 'What is wrong?'

Berenice folded her arms over her chest and said: 'Well, if you don't see it I can't explain it to you. Look there at your head, to begin with.'

F. Jasmine looked at her head in the mirror. 'You had all your hair shaved off like a convict, and now you tie a silver ribbon around this head without any hair. It just looks peculiar.'

'Oh, but I'm washing my hair tonight and going to try to curl it,' F. Jasmine said.

'And look at them elbows,' Berenice continued. 'Here you got on this grown woman's evening dress. Orange satin. And that brown crust on your elbows. The two things just don't mix.'

F. Jasmine hunched her shoulders and covered her rusty elbows with her hands.

Berenice gave her head another quick wide shake, then bunched her lips in judgement. 'Take it back down to the store.'

'But I can't!' said F. Jasmine. 'It's bargain basement. They don't take back.'

Berenice always had two mottoes. One was the known saying that you can't make a silk purse out of a sow's ear. And the other was the motto that you have to cut your suit according to the cloth, and make the best of what you have. So F. Jasmine was not certain if it was the last of these mottoes that made Berenice change her mind, or if she really began to improve her feelings about the dress. Anyway, Berenice stared for several seconds with her head to one side, and finally said:

'Come here. We'll make it fit better at the

waist and see what we can do.'

'I think you're just not accustomed to seeing anybody dressed up,' F. Jasmine said.

'I'm not accustomed to human Christmas trees in August.'

So Berenice took of the sash and patted and pulled the dress in various places. F. Jasmine stood stiff like a hat rack and let her work with the dress. John Henry had got up from his chair and was watching, with the napkin still tied around his neck.

'Frankie's dress looks like a Christmas tree,' he said.

'Two-faced Judas!' F. Jasmine said. 'You just now said it was pretty. Old double-faced Judas!'

The piano tuned. Whose piano it was F. Jasmine did not know, but the sound of the tuning was solemn and insistent in the kitchen, and it came from somewhere not so far away. The piano-tuner would sometimes fling out a rattling little tune, and then he would go back to one note. And repeat. And bang the same note in a solemn and crazy way. And repeat. And bang. The name of the piano-tuner in the town was Mr Schwarzenbaum. The sound was enough to shiver the gizzards of musicians and make all listeners feel queer.

'It almost makes me wonder if he does that just to torment us,' F. Jasmine said.

But Berenice said no: 'They tune pianos the same way in Cincinnati and the world over. It is just the way they do it. Less turn on the radio in the dining room and drown him out.'

F. Jasmine shook her head. 'No,' she said. 'I can't explain why. But I don't want to have that radio turned on again. It reminds me too much of this summer.'

'Step back a little now,' said Berenice.

She had pinned the waist higher and done one thing and another to the dress. F. Jasmine looked in the mirror over the sink. She could only see herself from the chest up, so after admiring this top part of herself, she stood on a chair and looked at the middle section. Then she began to clear away a corner of the table so she could climb up and see in the mirror the silver shoes, but Berenice prevented her.

'Don't you honestly think it is pretty?' F. Jasmine said. 'I think so. Seriously, Berenice. Give me your candy opinion.'

But Berenice rared up and spoke in an accusing voice: 'I never knew somebody so unreasonable! You ask me my candy opinion, and I give it to you. Then you ask me again, and I give it to you. But what you want is not my honest opinion, but my good opinion on something I know is wrong. Now what kind of way is that to act?'

'All right,' F. Jasmine said. 'I only want to look good.'

'Well, you look very well,' said Berenice. 'Pretty is as pretty does. You look well enough for anybody's wedding. Excepting your own. And then, pray Jesus, we will be in a position to do better. What I have to do now is get John Henry a fresh suit and figure about the outfit I'm going to wear myself.'

'Uncle Charles is dead,' John Henry said. 'And we are going to the wedding.'

'Yes, Baby,' said Berenice. And from the sudden dreaming quietness of her, F. Jasmine felt that Berenice was carried back to all the other dead people she knew. The dead were walking in her heart, and she was remembering back to Ludie Freeman and the long-gone time of Cincinnati and the snow.

F. Jasmine thought back to the other seven dead people she knew. Her mother had died the very day that she was born, so she could not count her. There was a picture of her mother in the right-hand drawer of her father's bureau: and the face looked timid and sorry, shut up with the cold folded handkerchiefs in the drawer. Then there was her grandmother who had died when Frankie was nine years old, and F. Jasmine remembered her very well – but with crooked little pictures that were sunken far back in her mind. A soldier from that town called William Boyd had been killed that year in Italy, and she had known him both by sight and name. Mrs Selway, two blocks away, had died; and F. Jasmine had watched the funeral from the sidewalk, but she was not invited. The solemn grown men stood around out on the front porch and it had rained, there was a grey silk ribbon on the door. She knew Lon Baker, and he was dead also. Lon Baker was a coloured boy and he was murdered in the alley out behind her father's store. On an April afternoon his throat was slashed with a razor blade, and all the alley people disappeared in back doorways, and later it was said his cut throat opened like a crazy shivering mouth that spoke ghost words into the April sun. Lon Baker was dead, and Frankie knew him. She knew, but only in a chancing kind of way, Mr Pitkin at Brawer's Shoe Shop, Miss Birdie Grimes, and a man who had climbed poles for the telephone company: all dead.

'Do you think very frequently about

Ludie?' F. Jasmine asked.

'You know I do,' said Berenice. 'I think about the years when me and Ludie was together, and about all the bad times I seen since. Ludie would never have let me be lonesome so that I took up with all kinds of no-good men. Me and Ludie,' she said. 'Ludie and me.'

F. Jasmine sat vibrating her leg and thinking of Ludie and Cincinnati. Of all the dead people out of the world, Ludie Freeman was the one F. Jasmine knew the best, although she had never laid eyes on him, and was not even born when he had died. She knew Ludie and the city of Cincinnati, and the winter when Ludie and Berenice had gone together to the North and seen the snow. A thousand times they had talked of all these things, and it was conversation that Berenice talked slowly, making each sentence like a song. And the old Frankie used to ask and question about Cincinnati. What exactly they would eat in Cincinnati and how wide would be the Cincinnati streets? And in a chanting kind of voice they talked about the Cincinnati fish, the parlour in the Cincinnati house on Myrtle Street, the Cincinnati picture shows. And Ludie Freeman was a brickmason, making a grand and regular salary, and he was the man of all her husbands that Berenice had loved.

'Sometimes I almost wish I had never knew Ludie at all,' said Berenice. 'It spoils you too much. It leaves you too lonesome afterward. When you walk home in the evening on the way from work, it makes a little lonesome quinch come in you. And you take up with too many sorry men to try to get over the feeling.'

'I know it,' F. Jasmine said. 'But T.T. Williams is not sorry.'

'I wasn't referring to T.T. He and me is just good friends.'

'Don't you think you will marry him?' F. Jasmine asked.

'Well, T.T. is a fine upstanding coloured gentleman,' said Berenice. 'You never hear tell of T.T. raring around like a lot of other mens. If I was to marry T.T., I could get out of this kitchen and stand behind the cash register at any restaurant and pat my foot. Furthermore, I respect T.T. sincerely. He has walked in a state of grace all of his life.'

'Well, when are you going to marry him?' she asked. 'He is crazy about you.'

Berenice said: 'I ain't going to marry him.'

'But you just now was saying–' said F. Jasmine.

'I was saying how sincerely I respect T.T. and sincerely regard him.'

'Well, then–?' F. Jasmine said.

'I respect and regard him highly,' said Berenice. Her dark eye was quiet and sober and her flat nose widened as she spoke. 'But he don't make me shiver none.'

After a moment F. Jasmine said: 'To think about the wedding makes me shiver.'

'Well, it's a pity,' said Berenice.

'It makes me shiver, too, to think about how many dead people I already know. Seven in all,' she said. 'And now Uncle Charles.'

F. Jasmine put her fingers in her ears and closed her eyes, but it was not death. She could feel the heat from the stove and smell the dinner. She could feel a rumble in her stomach and the beating of her heart. And the dead feel nothing, hear nothing, see nothing: only black.

'It would be terrible to be dead,' she said, and in the wedding dress she began to walk around the room.

There was a rubber ball on the shelf, and she threw it against the hall door and caught it on the rebound.

'Put that down,' said Berenice. 'Go take off the dress before you dirty it. Go do some-thing. Go turn on the radio.'

'I told you I don't want that radio on.'

And she was walking around the room, and Berenice had said to go do something, but she did not know what to do. She walked in the wedding dress, with her hand on her hip. The silver slippers had squeezed her feet so that the toes felt swollen and mashed like ten big sore cauliflowers.

'But I advise you to keep the radio on when you come back,' F. Jasmine said suddenly. 'Some day very likely you will hear us speaking over the radio.'

'What's that?'

'I say very likely we might be asked to speak over the radio some day.'

'Speak about what, pray tell me,' said Berenice.

'I don't know exactly what about,' F. Jasmine said. 'But probably some eye-witness account about something. We will be asked to speak.'

'I don't follow you,' said Berenice. 'What are we going to eye-witness? And who will ask us to speak?'

F. Jasmine whirled around and, putting both fists on her hips, she set herself in a staring position. 'Did you think I meant you and John Henry and me? Why, I have never heard of anything so funny in my whole life.'

John Henry's voice was high and excited. 'What, Frankie? Who is speaking on the radio?'

'When I said *we*, you thought I meant you and me and John Henry West. To speak over the world radio. I have never heard of anything so funny since I was born.'

John Henry had climbed up to kneel on the seat of his chair and the blue veins showed in his forehead and you could see the strained chords of his neck. 'Who?' he hollered. 'What?'

'Ha ha ha!' she said, and then she burst out laughing; she went banging around the room and hitting things with her fist. 'Ho ho ho!'

And John Henry wailed and F. Jasmine banged around the kitchen in the wedding dress and Berenice got up from the table and raised her right hand for peace. Then suddenly they all stopped at once. F. Jasmine stood absolutely still before the window, and John Henry hurried to the window also and watched on tiptoe with his hands to the sill. Berenice turned her head to see what had happened. And at that moment the piano was quiet.

'Oh!' F. Jasmine whispered.

Four girls were crossing the back yard.

They were girls of fourteen and fifteen years old, and they were the club members. First came Helen Fletcher, and then the others walking slowly in single file. They had cut across from the O'Neils' back yard and were passing slowly before the arbour. The long gold sun slanted down on them and made their skin look golden also, and they were dressed in clean, fresh dresses. When they had passed the arbour, their single shadows stretched out long and gangling across the yard. Soon they would be gone. F. Jasmine stood motionless. In the old days that summer she would have waited in the hope that they might call her and tell her she had been elected to the club – and only at the very last, when it was plain that they were only passing, she would have shouted in angry loudness that they were not to cut across her yard. But now she watched them quietly, without jealousy. At the last there came an urge to call out to them about the wedding, but before the words could be formed and spoken, the club of girls was gone. There was only the arbour and the spinning sun.

'Now I wonder–' F. Jasmine said finally. But Berenice cut her short:

'Nothing, Curiosity,' she said. 'Curiosity, nothing.'

When they began the second round of that last dinner, it was past five o'clock, and nearing twilight. It was the time of afternoon when in the old days, sitting with the red cards at the table, they would sometimes begin to criticize the Creator. They would judge the work of God, and mention the ways how they would improve the world. And Holy Lord God John Henry's voice would rise up happy and high and strange, and his world was a mixture of delicious and freak, and he did not think in global terms: the sudden long arm that could stretch from here to California, chocolate dirt and rains of lemonade, the extra eye seeing a thousand miles, a hinged tail that could be let down as a kind of prop to sit on when you wished to rest, the candy flowers.

But the world of the Holy Lord God Berenice Sadie Brown was a different world, and it was round and just and reasonable. First, there would be no separate coloured people in the world, but all human beings would be light brown colour with blue eyes and black hair. There would be no coloured people and no white people to make the coloured people feel cheap and sorry all through their lives. No coloured people, but all human men and ladies and children as one loving family on the earth. And when Berenice spoke of this first principle her voice was a strong deep song that soared and sang in beautiful dark tones leaving an echo in the corner of the room that trembled for a long time until silence.

No war, said Berenice. No stiff corpses hanging from the Europe trees and no Jews murdered anywhere. No war, and the young boys leaving home in army suits, and no wild cruel Germans and Japanese. No war in the whole world, but peace in all countries everywhere. Also, no starving. To begin with, the real Lord God had made free air and free rain and free dirt for the benefit of all. There would be free food for every human mouth, free meals and two pounds of fatback a week, and after that each able-bodied person would work for whatever else he wished to eat or own. No killed Jews and no hurt coloured people. No war and no hunger in the world. And, finally, Ludie Freeman would be alive.

The world of Berenice was a round world, and the old Frankie would listen to the strong deep singing voice, and she would agree with Berenice. But the old Frankie's world was the best of the three worlds. She agreed with Berenice about the main laws of her creation, but she added many things: an aeroplane and a motor-cycle to each person, a world club with certificates and badges, and a better law of gravity. She did not completely agree with Berenice about the war: and sometimes she said she would have one War Island in the world where those who wanted to could go, and fight or donate blood, and she might go for a while as a WAC in the Air Corps. She also changed the seasons, leaving out summer altogether, and adding much snow. She planned it so that people could instantly change back and forth from boys to girls, whichever way they felt like and wanted. But Berenice would argue with her about this, insisting that the law of human sex was exactly right just as it was and could in no way be improved. And then John Henry West would very likely add his two cents' worth about this time, and think that people ought to be half boy and half girl, and when the old Frankie threatened to take him to the Fair and sell him to the Freak Pavilion, he would only close his eyes and smile.

So the three of them would sit there at the kitchen table and criticize the Creator and the work of God. Sometimes their voices crossed and the three worlds twisted. The Holy Lord God John Henry West. The Holy

Lord God Berenice Sadie Brown. The Holy Lord God Frankie Addams. The worlds at the end of the long stale afternoons.

But this was a different day. They were not loafing or playing cards, but still eating dinner. F. Jasmine had taken off the wedding dress and was barefooted and comfortable in her petticoat once more. The brown gravy of the peas had stiffened, the food was neither hot nor cold, and the butter had melted. They started in on second helpings, passing the dishes back and forth among themselves, and they did not talk of the ordinary subjects that usually they thought about this time of the afternoon. Instead, there began a strange conversation, and it came about in this way:

'Frankie,' said Berenice, 'awhile back you started to say something. And we veered off from the subject. It was about something unnatural, I think.'

'Oh, yes,' F. Jasmine said. 'I was going to tell you about something peculiar that happened to me today that I don't hardly realize. Now I don't exactly know how to explain just what I mean.'

F. Jasmine broke open a sweet potato and tilted back in her chair. She began to try to tell Berenice what had happened when she had been walking home and suddenly seen something from the tail of her eye, and when she turned to look, it was the two coloured boys back at the end of the alley. As she talked, F. Jasmine stopped now and then to pull her lower lip and study just for the right words to tell of a feeling that she had never heard named before. Occasionally she glanced at Berenice, to see if she was following her, and a remarkable look was breaking on Berenice's face: the glass blue eye was bright and astonished, as always, and at first her dark eye was astonished also; then a queer and conniving look changed her expression, and from time to time she turned her head with short little jerks, as though to listen from different earpoints and make sure that what she heard was true.

Before F. Jasmine finished, Berenice had pushed back her plate and reached into her bosom for her cigarettes. She smoked home-rolled cigarettes, but she carried them in a Chesterfield package, so that from the outward appearance she was smoking store Chesterfields. She twisted off a ragged fringe of loose tobacco and raised back her head when she held the match, so that the flame would not go up her nose. A blue layer of smoke hung over the three of them at the table. Berenice held the cigarette between her thumb and forefinger; her hand had been drawn and stiffened by a winter rheumatism so that the last two fingers could not be straightened out. She sat listening and smoking, and when F. Jasmine had finished, there was a long pause, then Berenice leaned forward and asked suddenly:

'Listen at me! Can you see through them bones in my forehead? Have you, Frankie Addams, been reading my mind?'

F. Jasmine did not know what to answer.

'This is one of the queerest things I ever heard of,' Berenice went on. 'I cannot get over it.'

'What I mean–' F. Jasmine started again.

'I know what you mean,' said Berenice. 'Right here in this very corner of the eye.' She pointed to the red-webbed outside corner of the dark eye. 'You suddenly catch something there. And this cold shiver run all the way down you. And you whirl around. And then you stand facing Jesus knows what. But not Ludie and not who you want. And for a minute you feel like you been dropped down a well.'

'Yes,' F. Jasmine said. 'That is it.'

'Well, this is mighty remarkable,' said Berenice. 'This is a thing been happening to

166

me all my life. Yet just now is the first time I ever heard it put into words.'

F. Jasmine covered her nose and her mouth with her hand, so that it would not be noticed that she was pleased about being so remarkable, and her eyes were closed in a modest way.

'Yes, that is the way when you are in love,' said Berenice. 'Invariably. A thing known and not spoken.'

So that was how the queer conversation began at quarter to six on the last afternoon. It was the first time ever they had talked about love, with F. Jasmine included in the conversation as a person who understood and had worth-while opinions. The old Frankie had laughed at love, maintained it was a big fake, and did not believe in it. She never put any of it in her shows, and never went to love shows at the Palace. The old Frankie had always gone to the Saturday matinée, when the shows were crook shows, war shows, or cowboy shows. And who was it who had caused the confusion at the Palace that last May, when the movie had run an old show on Saturday called *Camille?* The old Frankie. She had been in her seat on the second row and she stamped and put two fingers in her mouth and began to whistle. And the other half-fare people in the first three rows began to whistle and stamp also, and the longer the love picture lasted, the louder they became. So that finally the manager came down with a flashlight and rooted the whole crowd of them out of their seats and marched them up the aisle and left them standing on the sidewalk: done out of their dimes, and disgusted.

The old Frankie had never admitted love. Yet here F. Jasmine was sitting at the table with her knees crossed, and now and then she patted her bare foot on the floor in an accustomed way, and nodded at what Berenice was saying. Furthermore, when she reached out quietly towards the Chesterfield package beside the saucer of melted butter, Berenice did not slap her hand away, and F. Jasmine took herself a cigarette. She and Berenice were two grown people smoking at the dinner table. And John Henry West had his big child head hunched close to his shoulder, watching and listening to all that went on.

'Now I will tell you a story,' said Berenice. 'And it is to be a warning to you. You hear me, John Henry? You hear me, Frankie?'

'Yes,' John Henry whispered. He pointed with his grey little forefinger. 'Frankie is smoking.'

Berenice sat up straight, her shoulders square, and her dark twisted hands folded before her on the table. She raised her chin and drew in her breath in the way of a singer who is beginning a song. The piano tuned and insisted, but when Berenice began to speak, her dark gold voice rang in the kitchen and they did not listen to the piano notes. But to start this warning Berenice began with the old same story that they had heard many times before. The story of her and Ludie Freeman. A long time ago.

'Now I am here to tell you I was happy. There was no human woman in all the world more happy than I was in them days,' she said. 'And that includes everybody. You listening to me, John Henry? It includes all queens and millionaires and first ladies of the land. And I mean it includes people of all colour. You hear me, Frankie? No human woman in all the world was happier than Berenice Sadie Brown.'

She had started with the old story of Ludie. And it began an afternoon in late October almost twenty years ago. The story started at the place where first they met each other, in front of Camp Campbell's Filling Station outside of the city limits of the town. It was the time of the year when the leaves were turning and the countryside was smoky and autumn grey and gold. And the story went on from that first meeting to the wedding at the Welcome Ascension Church in Sugarville. And then on through the years with the two of them together. The house with the brick front steps and the glass windows on the corner of Barrow Street. The Christmas of the fox fur, and the June of the fish fry thrown for twenty-eight invited relatives and guests. The years with Berenice cooking dinner and sewing Ludie's suits and shirts on the machine and the two of them always having a good time. And the nine months they lived up North, in the city of Cincinnati, where there was snow. Then Sugarville again, and days merging one into another, and the weeks, the months, the years together. And the pair of them always had a good time, yet it was not so much the happenings she mentioned as the way she told about these happenings that made F. Jasmine understand.

Berenice spoke in an unwinding kind of voice, and she had said that she was happier than a queen. As she told the story, it seemed to F. Jasmine that Berenice resembled a strange queen, if a queen can be coloured and sitting at a kitchen table. She unwound the story of her and Ludie like a coloured queen unwinding a bolt of cloth of gold – and at the end, when the story was over, her expression was always the same: the dark eye staring straight ahead, her flat nose widened and trembling, her mouth finished and sad and quiet. As a rule, when the story was over, they would sit for a moment and then suddenly get busy doing something in a hurry: start a hand of cards, or make milk-shakes, or just stir around the kitchen with no particular purpose. But this afternoon they did not move or speak for a long time after Berenice had finished, until finally F. Jasmine asked:

'What exactly did Ludie die of?'

'It was something similar to pneumonia,' said Berenice. 'November the year 1931.'

'The very year and the very month I was born,' F. Jasmine said.

'The coldest November I ever seen. Every morning there was frost and puddles were crusted with ice. The sunshine was pale yellow like it is in wintertime. Sounds carried far away, and I remember a hound dog that used to howl toward sundown. I kept a fire in the hearth going day and night, and in the evening when I walk around the room there was this shaking shadow following alongside of me on the wall. And everything I seen come to me as a kind of sign.'

'I think it is a kind of sign I was born the same year and the same month he died,' F. Jasmine said. 'Only the dates are different.'

'And then it was a Thursday toward six o'clock in the afternoon. About this time of day. Only November. I remember I went to the passage and opened the front door. We were living that year at 233 Prince Street. Dark was coming on, the old hound was howling far away. And I go back in the room and lay down on Ludie's bed. I lay myself down over Ludie with my arms spread out and my face on his face. And I pray that the Lord would contage my strength to him. And I ask the Lord let it be anybody, but not let it be Ludie. And I lay there and pray for a long time. Until night.'

'How?' John Henry asked. It was a question that did not mean anything, but he repeated it in a higher, wailing voce: 'How, Berenice?'

'That night he died,' she said. She spoke in a sharp tone, as though they had disputed with her. 'I tell you he died. Ludie! Ludie Freeman! Ludie Maxwell Freeman died!'

She was finished, and they sat there at the table. Nobody moved. John Henry stared at Berenice, and the fly that had been hovering above him lighted on the left rim of his glasses; the fly walked slowly across the left lens, and over the nosepiece, and across the right lens. It was only when the fly had flown away that John Henry blinked and waved his hand.

'One thing,' F. Jasmine said finally. 'There is Uncle Charles laying there dead right now. Yet somehow I can't cry. I know I ought to feel sad. Yet I feel sadder about Ludie than I do about Uncle Charles. Although I never laid eyes on Ludie. And I knew Uncle Charles all my life and he was blood kin to blood kin of mine. Maybe it's because I was born so soon after Ludie died.'

'Maybe so,' said Berenice.

It seemed to F. Jasmine that they might just sit there the rest of the afternoon, without moving or speaking, when suddenly she remembered something.

'You were starting out to tell a different story,' she said. 'It was some kind of warning.'

Berenice looked puzzled for a moment, then she jerked her head up and said: 'Oh, yes! I was going to tell you how this thing we was talking about applies to me. And what happened with them other husbands. Now you perk your ears.'

But the story of the other three husbands was an old story also. As Berenice began to talk, F. Jasmine went to the refrigerator and brought back to the table some sweetened condensed milk to pour on crackers as a desert. At first she did not listen very carefully.

'It was the April of the following year that I went one Sunday to the Forks Falls Church. And you ask what I was doing out there and I tell you. I was visiting that Jackson branch of my foster cousins who live out there and we had gone to their church. So there I was praying in this church where the congregation was strangers to me. I had my forehead down on the top of the pew in front of me, and my eyes were open – not gazing around in secret, mind you, but just open. When suddenly this shiver run all the way through me. I had caught sight of something from the corner of my eye. And I looked slowly to the left. And guess what I seen there? There on the pew, just six inches from my eye, was this *thumb*.'

'What thumb?' F. Jasmine asked.

'Now I'm telling you,' said Berenice. 'To understand this, you have to know that there was only one little portion of Ludie Freeman which was not pretty. Every other part about him was handsome and pretty as anyone would ever wish. All except his right thumb, which had been mashed in a hinge. This one thumb had a mashed chewed appearance that was not pretty. You understand?'

'You mean you suddenly saw Ludie's thumb when you were praying?'

'I mean I seen *this* thumb. And as I kneel there a shiver run from my head to my heels. I just kneel there staring at this thumb, and before I looked any further, to find out whose thumb it might be, I begun to pray in earnest. I prayed out aloud: Lord, manifest! Lord, manifest!'

'And did He?' F. Jasmine asked. 'Manifest?'

Berenice turned aside and made a sound like spitting. 'Manifest, my foot!' she said. 'You know who that thumb belonged to?'

'Who?'

'Why Jamie Beale,' said Berenice. 'That big old no-good Jamie Beale. It was the first time I ever laid eyes on him.'

'Is that why you married him?' F. Jasmine asked, for Jamie Beale was the name of the sorry old liquor-drinker, who was the second husband. 'Because he had a mashed thumb like Ludie's?'

'Jesus knows,' said Berenice. 'I don't. I felt drawn to him on account of the thumb. And then one thing led to another. First thing I knew I had married him.'

'Well, I think that was silly,' F. Jasmine said.

'To marry him just because of that thumb.'

'Me too,' said Berenice. 'I'm not trying to dispute with you. I'm just telling you what happened. And the very same thing occurred in the case of Henry Johnson.'

Henry Johnson was the third husband, the one who had gone crazy on Berenice. He was all right for three weeks after they had married, but then he went crazy, and he behaved in such a crazy way that finally she had to quit him.

'You mean to sit there and tell me Henry Johnson had one of those mashed thumbs too?'

'No,' said Berenice. 'It was not the thumb that time. It was the coat.'

F. Jasmine and John Henry looked at each other, for what she was saying did not seem to make much sense. But Berenice's dark eye was sober and certain, and she nodded to them in a definite way.

'To understand this, you have to know what happened after Ludie died. He had a policy due to pay off two hundred and fifty dollars. I won't go into the whole business, but what happened was that I was cheated by them policy people out of fifty dollars. And in two days I had to scour around and raise the fifty dollars to make out for the funeral. Because I couldn't let Ludie be put away cheap. I pawned everything I could lay hands on. And I sold my coat and Ludie's coat. To that second-hand clothing store on Front Avenue.'

'Oh!' F. Jasmine said. 'Then you mean Henry Johnson bought Ludie's coat and you married him because of it.'

'Not exactly,' said Berenice. 'I was walking down that street alongside of the City Hall one evening when I suddenly seen this shape before me. Now the shape of this boy ahead of me was so similar to Ludie through the shoulders and the back of the head that I almost dropped dead there on the sidewalk. I followed and run behind him. It was Henry Johnson, and that was the first time I ever saw him also, since he lived in the country and didn't come much into town. But he had chanced to buy Ludie's coat and he was built on the same shape as Ludie. And from the back view it looked like he was Ludie's ghost or Ludie's twin. But how I married him I don't exactly know, for to begin with it was clear that he did not have his share of sense. But you let a boy hang around and you get fond of him. Anyway, that's how I married Henry Johnson.'

'People certainy do curious things.'

'You telling me,' said Berenice. She glanced at F. Jasmine, who was pouring a slow ribbon of condensed milk over a soda cracker, to finish her dinner with a sweet sandwich.

'I swear, Frankie! I believe you got a tapeworm. I am perfectly serious. Your father looks over them big grocery bills and he naturally suspicions that I carry things off.'

'You do,' F. Jasmine said. 'Sometimes.'

'He reads over them grocery bills and he complains to me, Berenice, what in the name of holy creation did we do with six cans of condensed milk and forty-seven dozen eggs and eight boxes of marshmallows in one week. And I have to admit to him: Frankie eat them. I have to say to him: Mr Addams, you think you feeding something human back here in your kitchen. That's what you think. I have to say to him: Yes, you imagine it is something human.'

'After today I'm not going to be greedy any more,' F. Jasmine said. 'But I don't understand the point of what you was telling. I don't see how about that Jamie Beale and Henry Johnson applies to me.'

'It applies to everybody and it is a warning.'

'But how?'

'Why, don't you see what I was doing?' asked Berenice. 'I loved Ludie and he was

178

the first man I loved. Therefore, I had to go and copy myself forever afterward. What I did was to marry off little pieces of Ludie whenever I come across them. It was just my misfortune they all turned out to be the wrong pieces. My intention was to repeat me and Ludie. Now don't you see?'

'I see what you're driving at,' F. Jasmine said. 'But I don't see how it is a warning applied to me.'

'Then do I have to tell you?' asked Berenice.

F. Jasmine did not nod or answer, for she felt that Berenice had laid a trap for her, and was going to make remarks she did not want to hear. Berenice stopped to light herself another cigarette and two blue slow scrolls of smoke came from her nostrils and lazed above the dirty dishes on the table. Mr Schwarzenbaum was playing an arpeggio. F. Jasmine waited and it seemed a long time.

'You and that wedding at Winter Hill,' Berenice said finally. 'That is what I am warning about. I can see right through them two grey eyes of yours like they was glass. And what I see is the saddest piece of foolishness I ever knew.'

'Grey eyes is glass,' John Henry whispered.

But F. Jasmine would not let herself be

seen through and outstared; she hardened and tensed her eyes and did not look away from Berenice.

'I see what you have in your mind. Don't think I don't. You see something unheard of at Winter Hill tomorrow, and you right in the centre. You think you going to march down the centre of the aisle right in between your brother and the bride. You think you going to break into that wedding, and then Jesus knows what else.'

'No,' F. Jasmine said. 'I don't see myself walking down the centre of the aisle between them.'

'I see through them eyes,' said Berenice. 'Don't argue with me.'

John Henry said again, but softer: 'Grey eyes is glass.'

'But what I'm warning is this,' said Berenice. 'If you start out falling in love with some unheard-of thing like that, what is going to happen to you? If you take a mania like this, it won't be the last time and of that you can be sure. So what will become of you? Will you be trying to break into weddings the rest of your days? And what kind of life would that be?'

'It makes me sick to listen at people who don't have any sense,' F. Jasmine said, and she put her two fingers in her ears, but she did not push in the fingers very tight and she could still hear Berenice.

'You just laying yourself this fancy trap to catch yourself in trouble,' Berenice went on. 'And you know it. You been through the B section of the seventh grade and you are already twelve years old.'

F. Jasmine did not speak of the wedding, but her argument passed over it, and she said: 'They will take me. You wait and see.'

'And when they don't?'

'I told you,' F. Jasmine said. 'I will shoot myself with Papa's pistol. But they will take me. And we're never coming back to this part of the country again.'

'Well, I been trying to reason seriously,' said Berenice 'But I see it is no use. You determined to suffer,'

'Who said I was going to suffer?' F. Jasmine said.

'I know you,' said Berenice. 'You will suffer.'

'You are just jealous,' F. Jasmine said. 'You are just trying to deprive me of all the pleasure of leaving town. And kill the joy of it.'

'I am just trying to head this off,' said Berenice. 'But I see it is no use.'

John Henry whispered for the last time:

'Grey eyes is glass.'

It was past six o'clock, and the slow old afternoon began slowly to die. F. Jasmine took her fingers from her ears and breathed a long tired sigh. When she had sighed, John Henry sighed also, and Berenice concluded with the longest sigh of all. Mr Schwarzenbaum had played a ragged little waltz; but the piano was not yet tuned to suit him, and he began to harp and insist on another note. Again he played the scale up until the seventh note, and again he stuck there and did not finish. F. Jasmine was no longer watching the music with her eyes; but John Henry was watching, and when the piano stuck on the last note F. Jasmine could see him harden his behind and sit there stiff in the chair, his eyes raised, waiting.

'It is that last note,' F. Jasmine said. 'If you start with A and go on up to G, there is curious thing that seems to make the difference between G and A all the difference in the world. Twice as much difference as between any other two notes in the scale. Yet they are side by side there on the piano just as close together as the other notes. Do ray mee fa sol la tee. Tee. Tee. Tee. It could drive you wild.'

John Henry was grinning with his snaggle

teeth and giggling softly. 'Tee-tee,' he said, and he pulled at Berenice's sleeve. 'Did you hear what Frankie said? Tee-tee.'

'Shut your trap,' F. Jasmine said. 'Quit always being so evil-minded.' She got up from the table, but she did not know where to go. 'You didn't say anything about Willis Rhodes. Did he have a mashed thumb or a coat or something?'

'Lord!' said Berenice, and her voice was so sudden and shocked that F. Jasmine turned and went back to the table. 'Now that is a story would make the hair rise on your head. You mean to say I never told you about what happened with me and Willis Rhodes?'

'No,' F. Jasmine said. Willis Rhodes was the last and the worst of the four husbands, and he was so terrible that Berenice had had to call the Law on him. 'What?'

'Well, imagine this!' said Berenice. 'Imagine a cold bitter January night. And me laying all by myself in the big parlour bed. Alone in the house, because everybody else had gone for the Saturday night to Forks Falls. Me, mind you, who hates to sleep in a empty old bed all by myself and is nervous in a house alone. Past twelve o'clock on this cold bitter January night. Can you remember wintertime, John Henry?'

John Henry nodded.

'Now imagine this!' said Berenice again. She had begun stacking the dishes so that three dirty plates were piled before her on the table. Her dark eye circled around the table, roping in F. Jasmine and John Henry as her audience. F. Jasmine leaned forward, her mouth open and her hands holding the table edge. John Henry shivered down in his chair and he watched Berenice through his glasses without batting his eyes. Berenice had started in a low and creepy voice, then suddenly she stopped and sat there looking at the two of them.

'So what?' F. Jasmine urged, leaning closer across the table. 'What happened?'

But Berenice did not speak. She looked from one of them to the other, and shook her head slowly. Then when she spoke again her voice was completely changed, and she said: 'Why, I wish you would look yonder. I wish you would look.'

F. Jasmine glanced quickly behind her, but there was only the stove, the wall, the empty stair.

'What?' she asked. 'What happened?'

'I wish you would look,' Berenice repeated. 'Them two little pitchers and them four big ears.' She got up suddenly from the table.

'Come on, less wash the dishes. Then we going to make some cup cakes to take tomorrow on the trip.'

There was nothing F. Jasmine could do to show Berenice how she felt. After a long time, when the table before her was already cleared and Berenice stood washing dishes at the sink, she only said:

'If it's anything I mortally despise it's a person who starts out to tell something and works up people's interest and then stops.'

'I admit it,' said Berenice. 'And I am sorry. But it was just one of them things I suddenly realize I couldn't tell you and John Henry.'

John Henry was skipping and scuttling back and forth across the kitchen, from the stairway to the back porch door. 'Cup cakes!' he sang. 'Cup cakes! Cup cakes!'

'You could have sent him out of the room,' F. Jasmine said. 'And told me. But don't think I care. I don't care a particle what happened. I just wish Willis Rhodes had come in about that time and slit your throat.'

'That is a ugly way to talk,' said Berenice. 'Especially since I got a surprise for you. Go out on the back porch and look in the wicker basket covered with a newspaper.'

F. Jasmine got up, but grudgingly, and she walked in a crippled way to the back porch.

185

Then she stood in the doorway holding the pink organdie dress. Contrary to all that Berenice had maintained, the collar was pleated with tiny little pleats, as it was meant to be. She must have done it before dinner when F. Jasmine was upstairs.

'Well, this is mighty nice of you,' she said. 'I appreciate it.'

She would have liked for her expression to be split into two parts, so that one eye stared at Berenice in an accusing way, and the other eye thanked her with a grateful look. But the human face does not divide like this, and the two expressions cancelled out each other.

'Cheer up,' said Berenice. 'Who can tell what will happen? You might dress up in that fresh pink dress tomorrow and meet the cutest little white boy in Winter Hill you ever seen. It's just on such trips as these that you run into beaus.'

'But that's not what I'm talking about,' F. Jasmine said. Then, after a while, still leaning against the doorway, she added: 'Somehow we got off on the wrong kind of conversation.'

The twilight was white, and it lasted for a long while. Time in August could be divided

186

into four parts: morning, afternoon, twilight, and dark. At twilight the sky became a curious blue-green which soon faded to white. The air was soft grey, and the arbour and trees were slowly darkening. It was the hour when sparrows gathered and whirled about the rooftops of the town, and when in the darkened elms along the street there was the August sound of the cicadas. Noises at twilight had a blurred sound, and they lingered: the slam of a screen door down the street, voices of children, the whir of a lawn-mower from a yard somewhere. F. Jasmine brought in the evening newspaper, and dark was coming in the kitchen. The corners in the room at first were dark, then the drawings on the wall faded. The three of them watched the dark come on in silence.

'The army is now in Paris.'

'That's good.'

They were quiet awhile and then F. Jasmine said: 'I have a lot of things to do. I ought to start out now.'

But although she stood ready in the doorway, she did not go. On this last evening, the last time with the three of them together in the kitchen, she felt there was some final thing she ought to say or do before she went away. For many months she had been ready to leave this kitchen, never to return again; but now that the time had come, she stood there with her head and shoulder leaning against the door jamb, somehow unready. It was the darkening hour when the remarks they made had a sad and beautiful sound, although there would be nothing sad or beautiful about the meanings of the words.

F. Jasmine said quietly: 'I intend to take two baths tonight. One long soaking bath and scrub with a brush. I'm going to try to scrape this brown crust off my elbows. Then let out the dirty water and take a second bath.'

'That's a good idea,' said Berenice. 'I will be glad to see you clean.'

'I will take another bath,' John Henry said. His voice was thin and sad; she could not see him in the darkening room, since he stood in the corner by the stove. At seven Berenice had bathed him and dressed him in his shorts again. She heard him shuffle carefully across the room, for after the bath he had put on Berenice's hat and was trying to walk in Berenice's high-heeled shoes. Again he asked a question which by itself meant nothing. 'Why?' he asked.

'Why what, Baby?' said Berenice.

He did not answer, and it was F. Jasmine who finally said: 'Why is it against the law to change your name?'

Berenice sat in a chair against the pale white light of the window. She held the newspaper open before her, and her head was twisted down and to one side as she strained to see what was printed there. When F. Jasmine spoke, she folded the paper and put it away on the table.

'You can figure that out,' she said. 'Just because. Think of the confusion.'

'I don't see why,' F. Jasmine said.

'What is that on your neck?' said Berenice. 'I thought it was a head you carried on that neck. Just think. Suppose I would suddenly up and call myself Mrs Eleanor Roosevelt. And you would begin naming yourself Joe Louis. And John Henry would try to pass off as Henry Ford. Now what kind of confusion do you think that would cause?'

'Don't talk childish,' F. Jasmine said. 'That is not the kind of changing I mean. I mean from a name that doesn't suit you to a name you prefer. Like I changed from Frankie to F. Jasmine.'

'But still it would be a confusion,' Berenice insisted. 'Suppose we all suddenly change to entirely different names. Nobody would ever know who anybody was talking about. The whole world would go crazy.'

'I don't see—'

'Because things accumulate around your name,' said Berenice. 'You have a name and one thing after another happens to you, and you behave in various ways and do things, so that soon the name begins to have a meaning. Things have accumulated around the name. If it is bad and you have a bad reputation, then you just can't jump out of your name and escape like that. And if it is good and you have a good reputation, then you should be content and satisfied.'

'But what had accumulated around my old name?' F. Jasmine asked. Then, when Berenice did not reply at once, F. Jasmine answered her own question. 'Nothing! See? My name just didn't mean anything.'

'Well, that's not exactly so,' said Berenice. 'People think of Frankie Addams and it brings to the mind that Frankie is finished with the B section of the seventh grade. And Frankie found the golden egg at the Baptist Easter Hunt. And Frankie lives on Grove Street and—'

'But those things are nothing,' F. Jasmine said. 'See? They're not worth while. Nothing ever happened to me.'

'But it will,' said Berenice. 'Things will happen.'

'What?' F. Jasmine asked.

Berenice sighed and reached for the Chesterfield package inside her bosom. 'You pin me down like that and I can't tell you truthfully. If I could I would be a wizard. I wouldn't be sitting here in this kitchen right now, but making a fine living on Wall Street as a wizard. All I can say is that things will happen. Just what, I don't know.'

'By the way,' F. Jasmine said after a while. 'I thought I would go around to your house and see Big Mama. I don't believe in those fortunes, or anything like that, but I thought I might as well.'

'Suit yourself. However, I don't think it is necessary.'

'I suppose I ought to leave now,' F. Jasmine said.

But still she waited in the darkening door and did not go away. The sounds of the summer twilight crossed within the silence of the kitchen. Mr Schwarzenbaum had finished tuning the piano, and for the past quarter of an hour he had been playing little pieces. He played music memorized by note, and he was a nervous spry old man who reminded F. Jasmine of a silver spider. His music was spry and stiff also, and he played faint jerking waltzes and nervous lullabies. Farther

191

down the block a solemn radio announced something they could not hear. In the O'Neils' back yard, next door, children were calling and swatting a ball. The sounds of evening cancelled out each other, and they were faded in the darkening twilight air. The kitchen itself was very quiet.

'Listen,' F. Jasmine said. 'What I've been trying to say is this. Doesn't it strike you as strange that I am I, and you are you? I am F. Jasmine Addams. And you are Berenice Sadie Brown. And we can look at each other, and touch each other, and stay together year in and year out in the same room. Yet always I am I, and you are you. And I can't ever be anything else but me, and you can't ever be anything else but you. Have you ever thought of that? And does it seem to you strange?'

Berenice had been rocking slightly in the chair. She was not sitting in a rocking chair, but she had been tilting back in the straight chair, then letting the front legs hit the floor with little taps, her dark stiff hand held to the table edge for balance. She stopped rocking herself when F. Jasmine spoke. And finally she said: 'I have thought of it occasionally.'

It was the hour when the shapes in the kitchen darkened and voices bloomed. They spoke softly and their voices bloomed like flowers – if sounds can be like flowers and voices bloom. F. Jasmine stood with her hands clasped behind her head, facing the darkening room. She had the feeling that unknown words were in her throat, and she was ready to speak them. Strange words were flowering in her throat and now was the time for her to name them.

'This,' she said. 'I see a green tree. And to me it is green. And you would call the tree green also. And we would agree on this. But is this colour you see as green the same colour I see as green? Or say we both call a colour black. But how do we know that what you see as black is the same colour I see as black?'

Berenice said after a moment: 'Those things we just cannot prove.'

F. Jasmine scraped her head against the door, and put her hand up to her throat. Her voice shattered and died. 'That's not what I mean to say, anyway.'

The smoke of Berenice's cigarette lay bitter and warm and stagnant in the room. John Henry shuffled in the high-heeled shoes from the stove to the table and back again. A rat rattled behind the wall.

'This is what I mean,' F. Jasmine said. 'You are walking down a street and you meet somebody. Anybody. And you look at each other. And you are you. And he is him. Yet when you look at each other the eyes make a connexion. Then you go off one way. And he goes off another way. You go off into different parts of town, and maybe you never see each other again. Not in your whole life. Do you see what I mean?'

'Not exactly,' said Berenice.

'I'm talking about this town,' F. Jasmine said in a higher voice. 'There are all these people here I don't even know by sight or name. And we pass alongside each other and don't have any connexion. And they don't know me and I don't know them. And now I'm leaving town and there are all these people I will never know.'

'But who do you want to know?' asked Berenice

F. Jasmine answered: 'Everybody. In the world. Everybody in the world.'

'Why, I wish you would listen to that,' said Berenice. 'How about people like Willis Rhodes? How about them Germans? Them Japanese?'

F. Jasmine knocked her head against the door jamb and looked up at the dark ceiling. Her voice broke, and again she said: 'That's not what I mean. That's not what I'm talking about.'

'Well, what *is* you talking about?' asked Berenice.

F. Jasmine shook her head, almost as though she did not know. Her heart was dark and silent, and from her heart the unknown words flowered and bloomed and she waited to name them. From next door there was the evening sound of children's baseball and the long call: Batteruup! Batteruup! Then the hollow pock of a ball and the clatter of a thrown bat and running footsteps and wild voices. The window was a rectangle of pale clear light and a child ran across the yard and under the dark arbour after the ball. The child was quick as a shadow and F. Jasmine did not see his face – his white shirt-tails flapped loose behind him like queer wings. Beyond the window the twilight was lasting and pale and still.

'Less play out, Frankie,' John Henry whispered. 'They sound like they having a mighty good time.'

'No,' F. Jasmine said. 'You go.'

Berenice stirred in her chair and said: 'I suppose we could turn on the light.'

But they did not turn on the light. F. Jasmine felt the unsaid words stick in her throat and a choked sickness made her groan and knock her head against the door jamb. Finally she said again in a high ragged voice:

'This:'

Berenice waited, and when she did not speak again, she asked: 'What on earth is wrong with you?'

F. Jasmine could not speak the unknown words, so after a minute she knocked her head a last time on the door and then began to walk around the kitchen table. She walked in a stiff-legged delicate way, as she felt sick, and did not wish to joggle the different foods that she had eaten and mix them up inside her stomach. She began to talk in a high fast voice, but they were the wrong words, and not what she had meant to say.

'Boyoman! Manoboy!' she said. 'When we leave Winter Hill we're going to more places than you ever thought about or even knew existed. Just where we will go first I don't know, and it don't matter. Because after we go to that place we're going on to another. We mean to keep moving, the three of us. Here today and gone tomorrow. Alaska, China, Iceland, South America. Travelling on trains. Letting her rip on motor-cycles. Flying around all over the world in aeroplanes. Here today and gone tomorrow. All over the world. It's the damn truth. Boyoman!'

F. Jasmine jerked open the drawer of the table and fumbled inside for the butcher knife. She did not need the butcher knife, but she wanted something to grasp in her hand and wave about as she hurried around the table.

'And talking of things happening,' she said. 'Things will happen so fast we won't hardly have time to realize them. Captain Jarvis Addams sinks twelve Jap battleships and decorated by the President. Miss F. Jasmine Addams breaks all records. Mrs Janice Addams elected Miss United Nations in beauty contest. One thing after another happening so fast we don't hardly notice them.'

'Hold still, Fool,' said Berenice. 'And lay down that knife.'

'And we will meet them. Everybody. We will just walk up to people and know them right away. We will be walking down a dark road and see a lighted house and knock on the door and strangers will rush to meet us and say: Come in! Come in! We will know decorated aviators and New York people and movie-stars. We will have thousands of friends, thousands and thousands and thousands of friends. We will belong to so many clubs that we can't even keep track of all of them. We will be members of the whole world. Boyoman! Manoboy!'

Berenice had a very strong long right arm, and when F. Jasmine passed her the next time as she was running around the table, this arm reached out and snatched her by the petticoat so quickly that she was caught up with a jerk that made her bones crack and her teeth rattle.

'*Is* you gone raving wild?' she asked. The long arm pulled F. Jasmine closer and wrapped around her waist. 'You sweating like a mule. Lean down and let me feel your forehead. Is you got a fever?'

F. Jasmine pulled one of Berenice's plaits and pretended she was going to saw it off with the knife.

'You trembling,' said Berenice. 'I truly believe you took a fever walking round in that sun today. Baby, you sure you ain't sick?'

'Sick?' asked F. Jasmine. 'Who, me?'

'Set here in my lap,' said Berenice. 'And rest a minute.'

F. Jasmine put the knife on the table and settled down on Berenice's lap. She leaned back and put her face against Berenice's neck; her face was sweaty and Berenice's neck was sweaty also, and they both smelled salty and sour and sharp. Her right leg was flung across Bernice's knee, and it was trembling – but when she steadied her toes on the floor, her leg did not tremble anymore. John Henry shuffled towards them in the high-heeled shoes and crowded up jealous and close to Berenice. He put his arm around Berenice's head and held on to her ear. Then after a moment he tried to push F. Jasmine out of her lap, and he pinched F. Jasmine with a mean and tiny little pinch.

'Leave Frankie alone,' said Berenice. 'She ain't bothered you.'

He made a fretting sound: 'I'm sick.'

'Now no, you ain't. Be quiet and don't grudge your cousin a little bit of love.'

'Old mean bossy Frankie,' he complained in a high sad voice.

'What she doing so mean right now? She just laying here wore out.'

F. Jasmine rolled her head and rested her face against Berenice's shoulder. She could feel Berenice's soft big ninnas against her back, and her soft wide stomach, her warm solid legs. She had been breathing very fast, but after a minute her breath slowed down so that she breathed in time with Berenice; the two of them were close together as one body, and Berenice's stiffened hands were clasped around F. Jasmine's chest. Their backs were to the window, and before them the kitchen was now almost dark. It was Berenice who finally sighed and started the conclusion of that last queer conversation.

'I think I have a vague idea what you were driving at,' she said. 'We all of us somehow caught. We born this way or that way and we don't know why. But we caught anyhow. I born Berenice. You born Frankie. John Henry born John Henry. And maybe we wants to widen and bust free. But no matter what we do we still caught. Me is me and you is you and he is he. We each one of us somehow caught all by yourself. Is that what you was trying to say?'

'I don't know,' F. Jasmine said. 'But I don't want to be caught.'

'Me neither,' said Berenice. 'Don't none of us. I'm caught worse than you is.'

F. Jasmine understood why she had said this, and it was John Henry who asked in his child voice: 'Why?'

'Because I am black,' said Berenice. 'Because I am coloured. Everybody is caught one way or another. But they done drawn completely extra bounds around all coloured people. They done squeezed us off in one corner by ourself. So we caught that firstway I was telling you, as all human beings is caught. And we caught as coloured people also. Sometimes a boy like Honey feel like he just can't breathe no more. He feel like he got to break something or break himself. Sometimes it just about more than we can stand.'

'I know it,' F. Jasmine said. 'I wish Honey could do something.'

'He just feels desperate like.'

'Yes,' F. Jasmine said. 'Sometimes I feel like I want to break something, too. I feel like I wish I could just tear down the whole town.'

'So I have heard you mention,' said Berenice. 'But that won't help none. The point is that we all caught. And we try in one way or another to widen ourself free. For instance, me and Ludie. When I was with Ludie, I didn't feel so caught. But then Ludie died. We go around trying one thing or another, but we caught anyhow.'

The conversation made F. Jasmine almost afraid. She lay there close to Berenice and they were breathing very slowly. She could not see John Henry, but she could feel him; he had climbed up on the back rungs of the chair and was hugging Berenice's head. He was holding her ears, for in a moment Berenice said: 'Candy, don't wrench my ears like that. Me and Frankie ain't going to float up through the ceiling and leave you.'

Water dropped slowly into the kitchen sink and the rat was knocking behind the wall.

'I believe I realize what you were saying,' F. Jasmine said. 'Yet at the same time you almost might use the word loose instead of caught. Although they are two opposite words. I mean you walk around and you see all the people. And to me they look loose.'

'Wild, you mean?'

'Oh, no!' she said. 'I mean you don't see what joins them up together. You don't know where they all came from, or where they're going to. For instance, what made anybody ever come to this town in the first place? Where did all these people come from and what are they going to do? Think of all those soldiers.'

'They were born,' said Berenice. 'And they going to die.'

F. Jasmine's voice was thin and high. 'I know,' she said. 'But what is it all about? People loose and at the same time caught. Caught and loose. All these people and you don't know what joins them up. There's bound to be some sort of reason and con-nexion. Yet somehow I can't seem to name it. I don't know.

'If you did you would be God,' said Berenice. 'Didn't you know that?'

'Maybe so.'

'We just know so much. Then beyond that we don't know no more.'

'But I wish I did.' Her back was cramped and she stirred and stretched herself on Berenice's lap, her long legs sprawled out beneath the kitchen table. 'Anyway, after we leave Winter Hill I won't have to worry about things any more.'

'You don't have to now. Nobody requires you to solve the riddles of the world.' Berenice took a deep meaning breath and said: 'Frankie, you got the sharpest set of human bones I ever felt.'

This was a strong hint for F. Jasmine to stand up. She would turn on the light, then take one of the cup cakes from the stove, and go out to finish her business in the town. But for a moment longer she lay there with her face pressed close to Berenice's shoulder. The sounds of the summer evening were mingled and long-drawn.

'I never did say just what I was talking about,' she said finally. 'But there's this. I wonder if you have ever thought about this. Here we are – right now. This very minute. Now. But while we're talking right now, this minute is passing. And it will never come again. Never in all the world. When it is gone it is gone. No power on earth could bring it back again. It is gone. Have you ever thought about that?'

Berenice did not answer, and the kitchen was now dark. The three of them sat silent, close together, and they could feel and hear each other's breaths. Then suddenly it started, though why and how they did not know; the three of them began to cry. They started at exactly the same moment, in the way that often on these summer evenings they would suddenly start a song. Often in the dark, that August, they would all at once begin to sing a Christmas carol, or a song like the Slitbelly Blues. Sometimes they knew in advance that they would sing, and they would agree on the tune among themselves.

Or again, they would disagree and start off on three different songs at once, until at last the tunes began to merge and they sang a special music that the three of them made up together. John Henry sang in a high wailing voice, and no matter what he named his tune, it sounded always just the same: one high trembling note that hung like a musical ceiling over the rest of the song. Berenice's voice was dark and definite and deep, and she rapped the offbeats with her heel. The old Frankie sang up and down the middle space between John Henry and Berenice, so that their three voices were joined, and the parts of the song were woven together.

Often they would sing like this and their tunes were sweet and queer in the August kitchen after it was dark. But never before had they suddenly begun to cry; and though their reasons were three different reasons, yet they started at the same instant as though they had agreed together. John Henry was crying because he was jealous, though later he tried to say he cried because of the rat behind the wall. Berenice was crying because of their talk about coloured people, or because of Ludie, or perhaps because F. Jasmine's bones were really sharp. F. Jasmine did not know why she cried, but the reason she named was the crew-cut and the fact that her elbows were so rusty. They cried in the dark for about a minute. Then they stopped as suddenly as they had begun. The unaccustomed sound had quieted the rat behind the wall.

'Get up from there,' said Berenice. They stood around the kitchen table and F. Jasmine turned on the light. Berenice scratched her head and sniffled a little. 'We certainly is a gloomy crowd. Now I wonder what started that.'

The light was sudden and sharp after the darkness. F. Jasmine ran the faucet of the sink and put her head beneath the stream of water. And Berenice wiped off her face with a dishrag and patted her plaits before the mirror. John Henry stood like a little old woman dwarf, wearing the pink hat with the plume, and the high-heel shoes. The walls of the kitchen were crazy drawn and very bright. The three of them blinked at each other in the light as though they were three strangers or three ghosts. Then the front door opened and F. Jasmine heard her father trudging slowly down the hall. Already the moths were at the window, flattening their wings against the screen, and the final kitchen afternoon was over at last.

3

Early that evening F. Jasmine passed before the jail; she was on her way to Sugarville to have her fortune told and, though the jail was not directly on the way, she had wanted to have one final look at it before she left the town for ever. For the jail had scared and haunted her that spring and summer. It was an old brick jail, three stories high, and surrounded by a cyclone fence topped with barbed wire. Inside were thieves, robbers, and murderers. The criminals were caged in stone cells with iron bars before the windows, and though they might beat on the stone walls or wrench at the iron bars, they could never get out. They wore striped jail clothes and ate cold peas with cockroaches cooked in them and cold cornbread.

F. Jasmine knew some people who had been locked up in jail, all of them coloured – a boy called Cape, and a friend of Berenice who was accused by the white lady he worked for of stealing a sweater and a pair of shoes. When you were arrested, the Black Maria screamed to your house and a crowd of policemen burst in the door to haul you off down to the jail. After she took the three-bladed knife from the Sears and Roebuck store, the jail had drawn the old Frankie – and sometimes on those late spring afternoons she would come to the street across from the jail, a place known as Jail-Widow's Walk, and stare for a long time. Often some criminals would be hanging to the bars; it seemed to her that their eyes, like the long eyes of the Freaks at the fair, had called to her as though to say: We know you. Occasionally, on Saturday afternoon, there would be wild yells and singing and hollering from the big cell known as the Bull Pen. But now this evening the jail was quiet – but from a lighted cell there was one criminal, or rather the outline of his head and his two fists around the bars. The brick jail was gloomy dark, although the yard and some cells were lighted.

'What are you locked up for?' John Henry called. He stood at a little distance from F. Jasmine and he was wearing the jonquil dress, as F. Jasmine had given him all the costumes. She had not wished to take him with her; but he had pleaded and pleaded, and finally followed at a distance, anyway. When the criminal did not answer, he called again in a thin, high voice. 'Are you going to be hung?'

'Hush up!' F. Jasmine said. The jail did not frighten her this evening, for this time to-morrow she would be far away. She gave the jail a last glance and then walked on. 'How would you like for somebody to holler something like that to you if you were in jail?'

It was past eight o'clock when she reached Sugarville. The evening was dusty and lavender. Doors of the crowded houses on either side were open, and from some parlours there was the quavered flutter of oil lamps, lighting up the front-room beds and decorated mantelpieces. Voices sounded slurred and from a distance came the jazz of a piano and horn. Children played in alleyways, leaving whorled footsteps in the dust. The people were dressed for Saturday night, and on a corner she passed a group of jesting coloured boys and girls in shining evening dresses. There was a party air about the street that reminded her that she, also, could go that very evening to a date at the Blue Moon. She spoke to people on the street and felt again the unexplainable connexion between her eyes and other eyes. Mixed with the bitter dust, and smells of privies and supper-time, the smell of a clematis vine threaded the evening air. The house where Berenice lived was on the corner of Chinaberry Street – a two-room house with a tiny front yard bordered by shards and bottlecaps. A bench on the front porch held pots of cool, dark ferns. The door was only partly open and F. Jasmine could see the gold-grey flutters of the lamplight inside.

'You stay out here,' she said to John Henry.

There was the murmuring of a strong, cracked voice behind the door, and when F. Jasmine knocked, the voice was quiet a second and then asked:

'Who that? Who is it?'

'Me,' she said, for if she answered her true name, Big Mama would not recognize it. 'Frankie.'

The room was close, although the wooded shutter stood open, and there was the smell of sickness and fish. The crowded parlour was neat. One bed stood against the right wall, and on the opposite side of the room were a sewing machine and a pump organ. Over the hearth hung a photograph of Ludie Freeman; the mantelpiece was decorated with fancy calendars, fair prizes, souvenirs. Big Mama lay in the bed against the wall next to the door, so that in the day-time she could look out through the front window on to the ferny porch and street outside. She was an old coloured woman, shrivelled and with bones like broomsticks; on the left side of her face and neck the skin was the colour of tallow, so that part of her face was almost white and the rest copper-coloured. The old Frankie used to think that Big Mama was slowly turning to a white person, but Berenice had said it was a skin disease that sometimes happened to coloured people. Big Mama had done fancy washing and fluted curtains until the year the misery had stiffened her back so that she took to bed.

But she had not lost any faculties; instead, she suddenly found second-sight. The old Frankie had always thought she was uncanny, and when she was a little girl Big Mama was connected in her mind with the three ghosts who lived inside the coalhouse. And even now, a child no longer, she still had an eerie feeling about Big Mama. She was lying on three feather pillows, the covers of which were bordered with crochet, and over her bony legs there was a many-coloured quilt. The parlour table with the lamp was pulled up close beside the bed so that she could reach the objects on it: a dream-book, a white saucer, a workbasket, a jelly-glass of water, a Bible, and other things. Big Mama had been talking to herself before F. Jasmine came in, as she had the constant habit of telling herself just who she was and what she was doing and what she intended to do as she lay there in the bed. There were three mirrors on the walls which reflected the wavelike light from the lamp that fluttered gold-grey in the room and cast giant shadows; the lampwick needed trimming. Someone was walking in the back room.

'I came to get my fortune told,' F. Jasmine said.

While Big Mama talked to herself when

alone, she could be very silent at other times. She stared at F. Jasmine for several seconds before she answered: 'Very well. Draw up that stool before the organ.'

F. Jasmine brought the stool close to the bed, and leaning forward, stretched out her palm. But Big Mama did not take her palm. She examined F. Jasmine's face, then spat a wad of snuff into a chamberpot which she pulled from underneath the bed, and finally put on her glasses. She waited so long that it occurred to F. Jasmine that she was trying to read her mind, and this made her uneasy. The walking in the back room stopped and there was no sound in the house.

'Cast back your mind and remember,' she said finally. 'Tell me the revelation of your last dream.'

F. Jasmine tried to cast back her mind, but she did not dream often. Then finally she remembered a dream she had had that summer: 'I dreamed there was a door,' she said. 'I was just looking at it and while I watched, it began slowly to open. And it made me feel funny and I woke up.'

'Was there a hand in the dream?'

F. Jasmine thought. 'I don't think so.'

'Was there a cockroach on that door?'

'Why – I don't think so.'

'It signifies as follows.' Big Mama slowly closed and opened her eyes. 'There going to be a change in your life.'

Next she took F. Jasmine's palm and studied it for quite a while. 'I see here where you going to marry a boy with blue eyes and light hair. You will live to be your three-score and ten, but you must act careful about water. I see here a red-clay ditch and a bale of cotton.'

F. Jasmine thought to herself that there was nothing to it, only a pure waste of money and time. 'What does that signify?'

But suddenly the old woman raised her head and the cords of her neck stiffened as she called: 'You, Satan!'

She was looking at the wall between the parlour and the kitchen, and F. Jasmine turned to look over her shoulder also.

'Yessum,' a voice replied from the back room, and it sounded like Honey.

'How many times is I got to tell you to take them big feets off the kitchen table!'

'Yessum,' Honey said again. His voice was meek as Moses, and F. Jasmine could hear him put his feet down on the floor.

'Your nose is going to grow into that book, Honey Brown. Put it down and finish up your supper.'

F. Jasmine shivered. Had Big Mama looked clear through the wall and seen Honey reading with his feet up on the table? Could those eyes pierce through a pure plank wall? It seemed as though it would behove her to listen carefully to every word.

'I see here a sum of money. A sum of money. And I see a wedding.'

F. Jasmine's outstretched hand trembled a little. 'That!' she said. 'Tell me about that!'

'The wedding or the money?'

'The wedding.'

The lamplight made an enormous shadow of them on the bare boards of the wall. 'It's the wedding of a near relation. And I foresee a trip ahead.'

'A trip?' she asked. 'What kind of a trip? A long trip?'

Big Mama's hands were crooked, spotted with freckly pale blots, and the palms were like melted pink birthday candles. 'A short trip,' she said.

'But how—?' F. Jasmine began.

'I see a going and a coming back. A departure and a return.'

There was nothing to it, for surely Berenice had told her about the trip to Winter Hill and the wedding. But if she could see straight through a wall – 'Are you sure?'

'Well–' This time the old cracked voice was not so certain. 'I see a departure and a return, but it may not be for *now*. I can't guarantee. For at the same time I see roads, trains, and a sum of money.'

'Oh!' F. Jasmine said.

There was the sound of footsteps, and Honey Camden Brown stood on the threshold between the kitchen and the parlour. He wore tonight a yellow shirt with a bow tie, for he was usually a natty dresser – but his dark eyes were sad, and his long face still as stone. F. Jasmine knew what Big Mama had said about Honey Brown. She said he was a boy God had not finished. The Creator had withdrawn His hand from him too soon. God had not finished him, and so he had to go around doing one thing and then another to finish himself up. When she had first heard this remark, the old Frankie did not understand the hidden meaning. Such a remark put her in mind of a peculiar half-boy – one arm, one leg, half a face – a half-person hopping in the gloomy summer sun around the corners of the town. But later she understood it a little better. Honey played the horn, and had been first in his studies at the coloured high school. He ordered a French book from Atlanta and learned himself some French. At the same time he would suddenly run hog-wild all over Sugarville and tear around for several days, until his friends would bring him home more dead than living. His lips could move as light as butterflies and he could talk as well as any human she had ever heard – but other times he would answer with a coloured jumble that even his own family could not follow. The Creator, Big Mama said, had withdrawn His hand from him too soon, so that he was left eternally unsatisfied. Now he stood there leaning against the door jamb, bony and limp, and although the sweat showed on his face he somehow looked cold.

'Do you wish anything before I go?' he asked.

There was something about Honey that evening that struck F. Jasmine; it was as though, on looking into his sad, still eyes, she felt she had something to say to him. His skin in the lamplight was the colour of dark wistaria and the lips were quiet and blue.

'Did Berenice tell you about the wedding?' F. Jasmine asked. But, for once, it was not about the wedding that she felt she had to speak.

'Aaannh,' he answered.

'There's nothing I wish now. T.T. is due

here in a minute to visit with me for a while and meet up with Berenice. Where you off to, boy?'

'I'm going over to Forks Falls.'

'Well, Mr Up and Sudden, when you done decide that?'

Honey stood leaning against the door jamb, stubborn and quiet.

'Why can't you act like everybody else?' Big Mama said.

'I'll just stay over through Sunday and come back Monday morning.'

The feeling that she had something to say to Honey Brown still troubled F. Jasmine. She said to Big Mama: 'You were telling me about the wedding.'

'Yes.' She was not looking at F. Jasmine's palm, but at the organdie dress and the silk hose and the new silver slippers. 'I told you you would marry a light-haired boy with blue eyes. Later on.'

'But that's not what I'm talking about. I mean the other wedding. And the trip and what you saw about the roads and trains.'

'Exactly,' said Big Mama, but F. Jasmine had the feeling she was no longer paying much mind to her, although she looked again at her palm. 'I foresee a trip with a departure and a return and later a sum of money, roads, and trains. Your lucky number is six, although thirteen is sometimes lucky for you too.'

F. Jasmine wanted to protest and argue, but how could you argue with a fortune-teller? She wanted at least to understand the fortune better, for the trip with the return did not fit in with the foreseeing of roads and trains.

But as she was about to question further, there were footsteps on the front porch, a door knock, and T.T. came into the parlour. He was very proper, scraping his feet, and bringing Big Mama a carton of ice cream. Berenice had said he did not make her shiver, and it was true he was nobody's pretty man; his stomach was like a water-melon underneath his vest and there were rolls of fat on the back of his neck. He brought in with him the stir of company that she had always loved and envied about this two-room house. Always it had seemed to the old Frankie, when she could come here hunting Berenice, that there would be many people in the room – the family, various cousins, friends. In the wintertime they would sit by the hearth around the draughty, shivering fire and talk with woven voices. On clear autumn nights they were always the first to have sugar cane and Berenice would hack the joints of the slick, purple cane and they would throw the chewed, twisted pieces, marked with their teethprints, on a newspaper spread upon the floor. The lamplight gave the room a special look, a special smell.

Now, with the coming of T.T., there was the old sense of company and commotion. The fortune was evidently over, and F. Jasmine put a dime in the white china saucer on the parlour table – for, although there was no fixed price, the future-anxious folks who came to Big Mama usually paid what they felt due.

'I declare I never did see anybody grow like you do, Frankie,' Big Mama remarked. 'What you ought to do is tie a brickbat to your head.' F. Jasmine shrivelled on her heels, her knees bent slightly, and her shoulders hunched. 'That's a sweet dress you got on. And them silver shoes! And silk stockings! You look like a regular grown girl!'

F. Jasmine and Honey left the house at the same time, and she was still fretted by the feeling that she had something to say to him. John Henry, who had been waiting in the lane, rushed towards them, but Honey did not pick him up and swing him around as he sometimes did. There was a cold sadness about Honey this evening. The moonlight was white.

'What are you going to do in Forks Falls?'

'Just mess around.'

'Do you put any faith in those fortunes?' When Honey did not answer, she went on: 'You remember when she hollered back to you to take your feet off the table. Gave me a shock. How did she know your feet were on the table?'

'The mirror,' Honey said. 'She has a mirror by the door so she can see what goes on in the kitchen.'

'Oh,' she said. 'I never have believed in fortunes.'

John Henry was holding Honey's hand and looking up into his face. 'What are horsepowers?'

F. Jasmine felt the power of the wedding; it was as though, on this last evening, she ought to order and advise. There was something she ought to tell Honey, a warning or some wise advice. And as she fumbled in her mind, an idea came to her. It was so new, so unexpected, that she stopped walking and stood absolutely still.

'I know what you ought to do. You ought to go to Cuba or Mexico.'

Honey had walked on a few steps farther, but when she spoke he stopped also. John

Henry was midway between them, and as he looked from one to the other, his face in the white moonlight had a mysterious expression.

'Sure enough. I'm perfectly serious. It don't do you any good to mess around between Forks Falls and this town. I've seen a whole lot of pictures of Cubans and Mexicans. They have a good time.' She paused. 'This is what I'm trying to discuss. I don't think you will ever be happy in this town. I think you ought to go to Cuba. You are so light-skinned and you even have a kind of Cuban expression. You could go there and change into a Cuban. You could learn to speak the foreign language and none of those Cubans would ever know you are a coloured boy. Don't you see what I mean?'

Honey was still as a dark statue, and as silent.

'What?' John Henry asked again. 'What do they look like – them horsepowers?'

With a jerk Honey turned and went on down the lane. 'It is fantastic.'

'No, it is not!' Pleased that Honey had used the word fantastic to her, she said it quietly to herself before she went on to insist. 'It's not a particle fantastic. You mark my words. It's the best thing you can do.'

But Honey only laughed and turned off at the next alley. 'So long.'

The streets in the middle of the town reminded F. Jasmine of a carnival fair. There was the same air of holiday freedom; and, as in the early morning, she felt herself a part of everything, included and gay. On a Main Street corner a man was selling mechanical mice, and an armless beggar, with a tin cup in his lap, sat cross-legged on the sidewalk, watching. She'd never seen Front Avenue at night before, for in the evening she was supposed to play in the neighbourhood close to home. The warehouses across the street were black, but the square mill at the far end of the avenue was lighted in all its many windows and there was a faint mill humming and the smell of dyeing vats. Most of the businesses were open, and the neon signs made a mingling of varied lights that gave to the avenue a watery look. There were soldiers on corners, and other soldiers strolling along with grown date girls. The sounds were slurred late-summer sounds – footsteps, laughter, and above the shuffled noises, the voice of someone calling from an upper storey down into the summer street. The buildings smelled of sunbaked brick and the sidewalk was warm beneath the soles of her new silver shoes. F.

Jasmine stopped on the corner across from the Blue Moon. It seemed a long time since that morning when she had joined up with the soldier; the long kitchen afternoon had come between, and the soldier had somehow faded. The date, that afternoon, had seemed so very far away. And now that it was almost nine o'clock, she hesitated. She had the un-explainable feeling that there was a mistake.

'Where are we going?' John Henry asked. 'I think it's high time we went home.'

His voice startled her, as she had almost forgotten him. He stood there with his knees locked, big-eyed and drabbled in the tarlatan costume. 'I have business in town. You go home.' He stared up at her and took the bubble gum he had been chewing from his mouth – he tried to park the gum behind his ear, but sweat had made his ear too slippery, so finally he put the gum back in his mouth again. 'You know the way home as well as I do. So do what I tell you.' For a wonder, John Henry minded her; but, as she watched him going away from her down the crowded street, she felt a hollow sorriness – he looked so babyish and pitiful in the costume.

The change from the street to the inside of the Blue Moon was like the change that comes on leaving the open fairway and entering a booth. Blue lights and moving faces, noise. The counter and tables were crowded with soldiers, and men, and bright-faced ladies. The soldier she had promised to meet was playing the slot machine in a far corner, putting in nickel after nickel, but winning none.

'Oh, it's you,' he said when he noticed her standing at his elbow. For a second his eyes had the blank look of eyes that are peering back into the brain to recollect – but only for a second. 'I was scared you had stood me up.' After putting in a final nickel, he banged the slot machine with his fist. 'Let's find a place.'

They sat at a table between the counter and the slot machine, and, although by the clock the time was not long, it seemed to F. Jasmine endless. Not that the soldier wasn't nice to her. He was nice, but their two conversations would not join together, and underneath there was a layer of queerness she could not place and understand. The soldier had washed, and his swollen face, his ears and hands, were clean; his red hair was darkened from wetting and ridged with a comb. He said he had slept that afternoon. He was gay and his talk was sassy. But although she liked gay people and sassy talk, she could not think of any answers. It was again as though the soldier talked a kind of double-talk that, try as she would, she could not follow – yet it was not so much the actual remarks as the tone underneath she failed to understand.

The soldier brought two drinks to the table; after a swallow F. Jasmine suspected there was liquor in them and, although a child no longer, she was shocked. It was a sin and against the law for people under eighteen to drink real liquor, and she pushed the glass away. The soldier was both nice and gay, but after he had had two other drinks she wondered if he could be drunk. To make conversation she remarked that her brother had been swimming in Alaska, but this did not seem to impress him very much. Nor would he talk about the war, nor foreign countries and the world. To his joking remarks she could never find replies that fitted, although she tried. Like a nightmare pupil in a recital who has to play a duet to a piece she does not know, F. Jasmine did her best to catch the tune and follow. But soon she broke down and grinned until her mouth felt wooden. The blue lights in the crowded room, the smoke and noisy commotion, confused her also.

'You're a funny kind of girl,' the soldier said finally.

'Patton,' she said, 'I bet he will win the war in two weeks.'

The soldier was quiet now and his face had a heavy look. His eyes gazed at her with the same strange expression she had noticed that day at noon, a look she'd never seen on anyone before and could not place. After a while he said, and his voice was softened, blurred:

'What did you say your name is, Beautiful?'

F. Jasmine did not know whether or not to like the way he called her, and she spoke her name in a proper voice.

'Well, Jasmine, how bout going on upstairs?' His tone was asking, but when she did not answer at once, he stood up from the table. 'I've got a room here.'

'Why, I thought we were going to the Idle Hour. Or dancing or something.'

'What's the rush?' he said. 'The band don't hardly tune up until eleven o'clock.'

F. Jasmine did not want to go upstairs, but she did not know how to refuse. It was like going into a fair booth, or fair ride, that once having entered you cannot leave until the exhibition or the ride is finished. Now it was the same with this soldier, this date. She couldn't leave until it ended. The soldier was waiting at the foot of the stairs and, unable to refuse, she followed him. They went up two flights, and then along a narrow hall that smelled of wee-wee and linoleum. But every footstep F. Jasmine took, she felt somehow was wrong.

'This sure is a funny hotel,' she said.

It was the silence in the hotel room that warned and frightened her, a silence she noticed as soon as the door was closed. In the light of the bare electric bulb that hung down from the ceiling, the room looked hard and very ugly. The flaked iron bed had been slept in and a suitcase of jumbled soldier's clothes lay open in the middle of the floor. On the light oak bureau there was a glass pitcher full of water and a half-eaten package of cinnamon rolls covered with blue-white icing and fat flies. The screenless window was open and the sleazy voile curtains had been tied at the top in a knot together to let in air. There was a lavatory in the corner and, cupping his hands, the soldier dashed cold water to his face – the soap was only a bar of ordinary soap, already used, and over the lavatory a sign read: STRICTLY WASHING. Although the soldier's footsteps sounded, and the water made a trickling noise, the sense of silence somehow remained.

F. Jasmine went to the window which overlooked a narrow alley and a brick wall; a rickety fire-escape led to the ground and light shafted from the two lower storeys. Outside there was the August evening sounds of voices and a radio, and in the room there were sounds also – so how could the silence be explained? The soldier sat on the bed, and now she was seeing him altogether as a single person, not as a member of the loud free gangs who for a season roamed the streets of town and then went out into the world together. In the silent room he seemed to her unjoined and ugly. She could not see him any more in Burma, Africa, or Iceland, or even for that matter in Arkansas. She saw him only as he sat in the room. His light blue eyes, set close together, were staring at her with the peculiar look – with a filmed softness, like eyes that have been washed with milk.

The silence in the room was like that silence in the kitchen when, on a drowsy afternoon, the ticking of the clock would stop – and there would steal over her a mysterious uneasiness that lasted until she realized what was wrong. A few times before she had known such silence – once in the Sears and Roebuck store the moment before she suddenly became a thief, and again that April afternoon in the MacKeans' garage. It was the forewarning hush that comes before an unknown trouble, a silence caused, not by lack of sounds, but by a waiting, a suspense. The soldier did not take those strange eyes from her and she was scared.

'Come on, Jasmine,' he said, in an unnatural voice, broken and low, as he reached out his hand, palm upward, towards her. 'Let's quit this stalling.'

The next minute was like a minute in the fair Crazy House, or real Milledgeville. Already F. Jasmine had started for the door, for she could no longer stand the silence. But as she passed the soldier, he grasped her skirt and, limpened by fright, she was pulled down beside him on the bed. The next minute happened, but it was too crazy to be realized. She felt his arms around her and smelled his sweaty shirt. He was not rough, but it was crazier than if he had been rough – and in a second she was paralysed by horror. She could not push away, but she bit down with all her might upon what must have been the crazy soldier's tongue – so that he screamed out and she was free. Then he was coming towards her with an amazed pained face, and her hand reached the glass pitcher and brought it down upon his head. He swayed a second, then slowly his legs began to crumple, and slowly he sank sprawling to the floor. The sound was hollow like the hammer on a coconut, and with it the silence was broken at last. He lay there still, with the amazed expression on his freckled face that was now pale, and a froth of blood showed on his mouth. But his head was not broken, or even cracked, and whether he was dead or not she did not know.

The silence was over, and it was like those kitchen times when, after the first uncanny moments, she realized the reason for her uneasiness and knew that the ticking of the clock had stopped – but now there was no clock to shake and hold for a minute to her ear before she wound it, feeling relieved. There slanted across her mind twisted remembrances of a common fit in the front room, basement remarks, and nasty Barney; but she did not let these separate glimpses fall together, and the word she repeated was 'crazy'. There was water on the walls which had been slung out from the pitcher and the soldier had a broken look in the strewn room. F. Jasmine told herself: Get out! And after first starting towards the door, she turned and climbed out on the fire-escape and quickly reached the alley ground.

She ran like a chased person fleeing from the crazy-house at Milledgeville, looking neither to the right nor left, and when she reached the corner of her own home block, she was glad to see John Henry West. He was looking for bats around the street light, and the familiar sight of him calmed her a little.

'Uncle Royal has been calling you,' he said. 'What makes you shake like that for, Frankie?'

'I just now brained a crazy man,' she told him when she could get her breath. 'I brained him and I don't know if he is dead. He was a crazy man.'

John Henry stared without surprise. 'How did he act like?' And when she did not answer all at once, he went on: 'Did he crawl on the ground and moan and slobber?' For that was what the old Frankie had done one day to try to fool Berenice and create some excitement. Berenice had not been fooled. 'Did he?'

'No,' F. Jasmine said. 'He–' But as she looked into those cold, child eyes she knew that she could not explain. John Henry would not understand, and his green eyes gave her a funny feeling. Sometimes his mind was like the pictures he drew with crayons on tablet paper. The other day he had drawn such a one and showed it to her. It was a picture of a telephone man on a telephone pole. The telephone man was leaning against his safety belt, and the picture was complete down to his climbing shoes. It was a careful picture but after she had looked at it uneasiness had lingered in her mind. She looked at the picture again until she realized what was wrong. The telephone man was drawn in side-view profile, yet this profile had two eyes – one eye just above the nose bridge and another drawn just below. And it was no hurried mistake; both eyes had careful lashes, pupils, and lids. Those two eyes drawn in a side-view face gave her a funny feeling. But reason with John Henry, argue with him? You might as well argue with cement. Why did he do it? Why? Because it was a telephone man. What? Because he was climbing the pole. It was impossible to understand his point of view. And he did not understand her either.

'Forget what I just now told you,' she said. But after saying it, she realized that was the worst remark she could've said, for he would be sure not to forget. So she took him by the shoulders and shook him slightly. 'Swear you won't tell. Swear this: If I tell I hope God will sew up my moth and sew down my eyes and cut off my ears with the scissors.'

But John Henry would not swear; he only hunched his big head down near his shoulders and answered, very quietly: 'Shoo.'

She tried again. 'If you tell anybody I might

be put in jail and we couldn't go to the wedding.'

'I ain't going to tell,' John Henry said. Sometimes he could be trusted, and other times not. 'I'm not a tattletale.'

Once inside the house, F. Jasmine locked the front door before she went into the living-room. Her father was reading the evening paper, in his sock feet, on the sofa. F. Jasmine was glad to have her father between her and the front door. She was afraid of the Black Maria and listened anxiously.

'I wish we were going to the wedding right this minute,' she said. 'I think that would be the best thing to do.'

She went back to the icebox and ate six tablespoons of sweetened condensed milk, and the disgust in her mouth began to go away. The waiting made her feel restless. She gathered up the library books, and stacked them on the living-room table. On one of them, a book from the grown sections which she had not read, she wrote in the front with pencil: *If you want to read something that will shock you, turn to page 66.* On page 66 she wrote: *Electricity. Ha! Ha!* By and by her anxiousness was eased; close to her father she felt less afraid.

'These books are to go back to the library.'

Her father, who was forty-one, looked at the clock: 'It's time for everybody under forty-one to get to bed. Quick march, and without any argument. We have to be up at five o'clock.'

F. Jasmine stood in the doorway, unable to leave. 'Papa,' she said, 'if somebody hits somebody with a glass pitcher and he falls out cold, do you think he is dead?'

She had to repeat the question, feeling a bitter grudge against him because he did not take her seriously, so that her questions must be asked twice.

'Why, come to think about it, I never hit anybody with a pitcher,' he said. 'Did you?'

F. Jasmine knew he asked this as a joke, so she only said as she went away: 'I'll never be so glad to get to any place in all my life as Winter Hill tomorrow. I will be so thankful when the wedding is over and we have gone away. I will be so thankful.'

Upstairs she and John Henry undressed, and after the motor and the light were off, they lay down on the bed together – although she said she could not sleep a wink. But nevertheless she closed her eyes, and when she opened them again a voice was calling and the room was early grey.

PART III

She said: 'Farewell, old ugly house,' as, wearing a dotted Swiss dress and carrying the suitcase, she passed through the hall at quarter to six. The wedding dress was in the suitcase, ready to be put on when she reached Winter Hill. At that still hour the sky was the dim silver of a mirror, and beneath it the grey town looked, not a real town, but like an exact reflection of itself, and to this unreal town she also said farewell. The bus left the station at ten past six – and she sat proud, like an accustomed traveller, apart from her father, John Henry, and Berenice. But after a while a serious doubt came in her, which even the answers of the bus-driver could not quite satisfy. They were supposed to be travelling north, but it seemed to her rather that the bus was going south instead. The sky turned burning pale and the day blazed. They passed the fields of windless corn that had a blue look in the glare, red-furrowed cotton land, stretches of black pine woods. And mile by mile the countryside became more southern. The towns they passed – New City, Leeville, Cheehaw – each town seemed smaller than the one before, until at nine o'clock they reached the ugliest place of all, where they changed buses, called Flowering Branch. Despite its name there were no flowers and no branch – only a solitary country store, with a sad old shredded circus poster on the clapboard wall and a chinaberry tree beneath which stood an empty wagon and a sleeping mule. There they waited for the bus to Sweet Well, and, still doubting anxiously, Frances did not despise the box of lunch that had so shamed her at the first, because it made them look like family people who do not travel very much. The bus left at ten o'clock, and they were in Sweet Well by eleven. The next hours were unexplainable. The wedding was like a dream, for all that came about occurred in a world beyond her power; from the moment when, sedate and proper, she shook hands with the grown people until the time, the wrecked wedding over, when she watched the car with the two of them driving away from her, and, flinging herself down in the sizzling dust, she cried out for the last time: 'Take me! Take me!' – from the beginning to the end the wedding was unmanaged as a nightmare. By mid-afternoon it was all finished and the return bus left at four o'clock.

'The show is over and the monkey's dead,' John Henry quoted, as he settled himself in the next to the last bus seat beside her father. 'Now we go home and go to bed.'

Frances wanted the whole world to die. She sat on the back seat, between the window and Berenice, and, though she was no longer sobbing, the tears were like two little brooks, and also her nose ran water. Her shoulders were hunched over her swollen heart and she no longer wore the wedding dress. She was sitting next to Berenice, back with the coloured people, and when she thought of it she used the mean word she had never used before, nigger – for now she hated everyone and wanted only to spite and shame. For John Henry West the wedding had only been a great big show, and he had enjoyed her misery at the end as he had enjoyed the angel cake. She mortally despised him, dressed in his best white suit, now stained with strawberry ice cream. Berenice she hated also, for to her it had only meant a pleasure trip to Winter Hill. Her father, who had said that he would attend to her when they got home, she would like to kill. She was against every single person, even strangers in the crowded bus, though she only saw them blurred by tears – and she wished the bus would fall in a river or run into a train. Herself she hated the worst of all, and she wanted the whole world to die.

'Cheer up,' said Berenice. 'Wipe your face, and blow your nose and things will look better by and by.'

Berenice had a blue party handkerchief, to match her blue dress and blue kid shoes – and this she offered to Frances, although it was made of fine georgette and not of course, due to be blown on. She would not notice it. In the seat between them there were three wet handkerchiefs of her father's, and Berenice began to dry the tears with one, but Frances did not move or budge.

'They put old Frankie out of the wedding.' John Henry's big head bobbed over the back of his seat, smiling and snaggle-toothed. Her father cleared his throat and said: 'That's sufficient, John Henry. Leave Frankie alone.' And Berenice added: 'Sit down in that seat now and behave.'

The bus rode for a long time, and now direction made no difference to her; she did not care. From the beginning the wedding had been queer like the card games in the kitchen the first week last June. In those

238

bridge games they played and played for many days, but nobody ever drew a good hand, the cards were all sorry, and no high bids made – until finally Berenice suspicioned, saying: 'Less us get busy and count these old cards.' And they got busy and counted the old cards, and it turned out the jacks and the queens were missing. John Henry at last admitted that he had cut out the jacks and then the queens to keep them company and, after hiding the clipped scraps in the stove, had secretly taken the pictures home. So the fault of the card game was discovered. But how could the failure of the wedding be explained?

The wedding was all wrong, although she could not point out single faults. The house was a neat brick house out near the limits of the small, baked town, and when she first put foot inside, it was as though her eyeballs had been slightly stirred; there were mixed impressions of pink roses, the smell of floor wax, mints and nuts in silver trays. Everybody was lovely to her. Mrs Williams wore a lace dress, and she asked F. Jasmine two times what grade she was in at school. But she asked, also, if she would like to play out on the swing before the wedding, in the tone grown people use when speaking to a child.

Mr Williams was nice to her, too. He was a sallow man with folds in his cheeks and the skin beneath his eyes was the grain and colour of an old apple core. Mr Williams also asked her what grade she was in at school; in fact, that was the main question asked her at the wedding.

She wanted to speak to her brother and the bride, to talk to them and tell them of her plans, the three of them alone together. But they were never once alone; Jarvis was out checking the car someone was lending for the honeymoon, while Janice dressed in the front bedroom among a crowd of beautiful grown girls. She wandered from one to the other of them, unable to explain. And once Janice put her arms around her, and said she was so glad to have a little sister – and when Janice kissed her, F. Jasmine felt an aching in her throat and could not speak. Jarvis, when she went to find him in the yard, lifted her up in a rough-house way and said: 'Frankie the lankie the alaga fankie, the tee-legged toe-legged bow-legged Frankie.' And he gave her a dollar.

She stood in the corner of the bride's room, wanting to say: I love the two of you so much and you are the we of me. Please take me with you from the wedding, for we

240

belong to be together. Or even if she could have said: May I trouble you to step into the next room, as I have something to reveal to you and Jarvis? And get the three of them in a room alone together and somehow manage to explain. If only she had written it down on the typewriter in advance, so that she could hand it to them and they would read! But this she had not thought to do, and her tongue was heavy in her mouth and dumb. She could only speak in a voice that shook a little – to ask where was the veil?

'I can feel in the atmosphere a storm is brewing,' said Berenice. 'These two crooked joints can always tell.'

There was no veil except a little veil that came down from the wedding hat, and nobody was wearing fancy clothes. The bride was wearing a day-time suit. The only mercy of it was that she had not worn her wedding dress on the bus, as she had first intended, and found it out in time. She stood in a corner of the bride's room until the piano played the first notes of the wedding march. They were all lovely to her at Winter Hill, except that they called her Frankie and treated her too young. It was so unlike what she had expected, and, as in those June card games, there was, from first to last, the sense of something terribly gone wrong.

'Perk up,' said Berenice. 'I'm planning a big surprise for you. I'm just sitting here planning. Don't you want to know what it is?'

Frances did not answer even by a glance. The wedding was like a dream outside her power, or like a show unmanaged by her in which she was supposed to have no part. The living-room was crowded with Winter Hill company, and the bride and her brother stood before the mantelpiece at the end of the room. And seeing them again together was more like singing feeling than a picture that her dizzied eyes could truly see. She watched them with her heart, but all the time she was only thinking: I have not told them and they don't know. And knowing this was heavy as a swallowed stone. And afterwards, during the kissing of the bride, refreshments served in the dining-room, the stir and party bustle – she hovered close to the two of them, but words would not come. They are not going to take me, she was thinking, and this was the one thought she could not bear.

When Mr Williams brought their bags, she hastened after with her own suitcase. The rest was like some nightmare show in which a wild girl in the audience breaks on to the stage to take upon herself an unplanned part that was never written or meant to be. You are the we of me, her heart was saying, but she could only say aloud: 'Take me!' And they pleaded and begged with her, but she was already in the car. At the last she clung to the steering wheel until her father and somebody else had hauled and dragged her from the car, and even then she could only cry in the dust of the empty road: 'Take me! Take me!' But there was only the wedding company to hear, for the bride and her brother had driven away.

Berenice said: 'School will begin now in only three more weeks. And you'll go into the A section of the seventh grade and meet a lot of nice new children and make another bosom friend like that Evelyn Owen you were so wild about.'

The kind tone Frances could not stand. 'I never meant to go with them!' she said. 'It was all just a joke. They said they were going to invite me to visit when they get settled, but I wouldn't go. Not for a million dollars.'

'We know all about that,' said Berenice. 'Now listen to my surprise I've planned. Soon as you get settled in school and have a chance to make these friends, I think it would be a good idea to have a party. A lovely bridge party in the living-room, with potato salad and those little olive sand-wiches your Aunt Pet had for a club meeting you were so carried away about – the round-shaped kind with the tiny round hole in the middle and the olive showing. A lovely bridge party with delicious refreshments. How would you like that?'

The baby promises rasped her nerves. Her cheap heart hurt, and she pressed her crossed arms over it and rocked a little. It was a framed game. The cards were stacked. It was a frame-up all around.

'We can have that bridge party going on in the living-room. And out in the back yard we can have another party at the same time. A costume party with hot dogs. One party dainty and the other one rough. With prizes for the highest bridge score and the funniest costume. How does that strike you?'

Frances refused to look at Berenice or answer.

'You could call up the society editor of the *Evening Journal* and have the party written up in the paper. And that would make the fourth time your name has been published in the paper.'

It would, but a thing like that no longer mattered to her. Once, when her bike ran into an automobile, the paper had called her

Fankie Addams. *Fankie!* But now she did not care.

'Don't be so blue,' said Berenice. 'This is not doomsday.'

'Frankie, don't cry,' John Henry said. 'We will go home and put up the tepee and have a good time.'

She could not stop crying and the sobbing had a strangled sound. 'Oh, hush up your mouth!'

'Listen to me. Tell me what you would like and I'll try to do it if it's in my power.'

'All I would like,' said Frances, after a minute, 'all I would wish in the world, is for no human being ever to speak to me so long as I live.'

And Berenice said, finally: 'Well. Then bawl, then, Misery.'

They did not talk the rest of the way back to the town. Her father slept with a handkerchief over his nose and eyes, snoring a little. John Henry West lay in her father's lap and slept also. The other passengers were drowsy quiet and the bus rocked like a cradle and made a softly roaring sound. Outside the afternoon shimmered and now and then there was a buzzard lazily balanced against the blazing pale sky. They passed red empty crossroads with deep red gulches on either side, and rotten grey shacks set in the lonesome cotton fields. Only the dark pine trees looked cool – and the low blue hills when seen from miles away. Frances watched from the window with a stiff sick face and for four hours did not say a word. They were entering the town, and a change came. The sky lowered and turned a purple-grey against which the trees were a poison green. There was a jellied stillness in the air and then the mutter of the first thunder. A wind came through the treetops with a sound like rushing water, forewarning storm.

'I told you so,' said Berenice, and she was not speaking of the wedding. 'I could feel the misery in these joints. After a good storm we will all feel much better.'

The rain did not come, and there was only a feeling of expectation in the air. The wind was hot. Frances smiled a little at Berenice's words, but it was a scorning smile that hurt.

'You think it's all over,' she said, 'but that only shows how little you know.'

They thought it was finished, but she would show them. The wedding had not included her, but she would still go into the world. Where she was going she did not know; however, she was leaving town that night. If

246

she could not go in the way she had planned, safe with her brother and the bride, she would go, anyway. Even if she had to commit every crime. For the first time since the night before she thought about the solider – but only in a glancing way, for her mind was busy with hasty plans. There was a train that passed through the town at two o'clock, and she would take it; the train went north in a general way, probably to Chicago or New York. If the train went to Chicago, she would go on to Hollywood and write shows or get a job as a movie starlet – or, if worse came to worse, even act in comedies. If the train went to New York, she would dress like a boy and give a false name and a false age and join the Marines. Meanwhile, she had to wait until her father was asleep, and she could still hear him moving in the kitchen. She sat at the typewriter and wrote a letter.

Dear Father:
This is a farewell letter until I write you from a different place. I told you I was going to leave town because it is inevitable. I cannot stand this existence any longer because my life has become a burden. I am taking the pistol because who can tell when it might come in handy and I will send back the

money to you at the very first opportunity. Tell Berenice not to worry. The whole thing is a irony of fate and it is inevitable. Later I will write. Please Papa do not try to capture me.

Sincerely yours,
Frances Addams

The green-and-white moths were nervous at the window screen and the night outside was queer. The hot wind had stopped and the air was so still that it seemed solid and there was a weight against you when you moved. The thunder grumbled low occasionally. Frances sat motionless before the typewriter, wearing the dotted Swiss dress, and the strapped suitcase was beside the door. After a while the light in the kitchen was turned off and her father called from the foot of the stairs: 'Good night, Pickle-priss. Good night, John Henry.'

Frances waited a long time. John Henry was sleeping across the foot of the bed, still dressed and with his shoes on, and his mouth was open and one ear of his glasses frame had come loose. After waiting as long as she could stand it, she took the suitcase and tiptoed very quietly down the stairs. It was dark down there, dark in her father's room, dark through the house. She stood on the threshold of her father's room and he was snoring softly. The hardest time was the few minutes she stood there, listening.

The rest was easy. Her father was a widowman, set in his ways, and at night he folded his pants over a straight chair and left his wallet, watch, and glasses on the right-hand side of the bureau. She moved very quietly in the darkness and laid hand on the wallet almost immediately. She was careful opening the bureau drawer, stopping to listen each time there was a scraping sound. The pistol felt heavy and cool in her hot hand. It was easy except for the loudness of beating heart and for an accident that happened just as she crept from the room. She stumbled over a wastepaper basket and the snoring stopped. Her father stirred, muttered. She held her breath – then finally, after a minute, the snoring went on again.

She put the letter on the table and tiptoed to the back porch. But there was one thing she had not counted on – John Henry began to call.

'Frankie!' The high child voice seemed to carry through all the rooms of the night house. 'Where are you?'

'Hush,' she whispered. 'Go back to sleep.'

She had left the light on in her room, and he stood in the stairway door and looked down into the dark kitchen. 'What are you doing down there in the dark?'

'Hush!' she said again in a loud whisper. 'I'll be there by the time you get to sleep.'

She waited a few minutes after John Henry had gone, then groped to the back door, unlocked it, and stepped outside. But, though she was very quiet, he must have heard her. 'Wait, Frankie!' he wailed. 'I'm coming.'

The child wailing had waked her father, and she knew it before she reached the corner of the house. The night was dark and heavy, and as she ran, she heard her father calling her. Behind the corner of the house she looked and saw the kitchen light go on; the bulb swung back and forth, making a swinging gold reflection on the arbour and the dark yard. He will read the letter now, she thought, and chase and try to capture me. But after she had run a few blocks, the suitcase bumping against her legs and sometimes nearly tripping her, she remembered that her father would have to put on pants and a shirt – for he would not chase her through the streets dressed only in pyjama bottoms. She stopped for a second to look behind. No one was there. At the first street light she put down the suitcase and, taking the wallet from the front pocket of her dress, opened it with shaking hands. Inside there was three dollars and fifteen cents. She would have to hop a box car, or something.

All at once, alone there in the night-empty street, she realized she did not know how. It is easy to talk about hopping a freight train, but how did bums and people really do it? She was three blocks from the station and she walked towards it slowly. The station was closed and she went round it and stared at the platform, long and empty under the pale lights, with the Chiclet machines against the station wall and scraps of chewing-gum paper and candy wrappings on the platform. The train tracks gleamed silver and exact and some freight cars were off on a siding in the distance, but they were not hooked to any engine. The train would not come until two o'clock, and would she be able to hop a car, as she had read about, and get away! There was a red lantern a little way down the tracks, and against this coloured light she saw a railroad man come walking slowly. She could not hang around like that until two o'clock – but as she left the station, one shoulder dragged down by the weight of the bag, she did not know where she should go.

The streets were lonesome and idle with Sunday night. The red-and-green neon lights in the sign-boards mixed with the street lights to make a pale hot haze above the town, but the sky was starless, black. A man in a tilted hat took out his cigarette and turned to stare at her as she passed by. She could not wander around the town like this, for by this time her father would be chasing her. In the alley behind Finny's Place she sat down on the suitcase, and only then she realized that the pistol was still in her left hand. She had been going around with a pistol held right in her hand, and she felt that she had lost her mind. She had said that she would shoot herself if the bride and her brother would not take her. She pointed the pistol at the side of her head and held it there a minute or two. If she squeezed down on the trigger she would be dead – and deadness was blackness, nothing but pure terrible blackness that went on and on and never ended until the end of all the world. When she lowered the pistol, she told herself that at the last minute she had changed her mind. The pistol she put in her suitcase.

The alley was black and smelled of garbage cans, and it was in this alley where Lon Baker had his throat slashed that spring afternoon so that his neck was like a bloody mouth that gibbered in the sun. It was here Lon Baker had been killed. And had she killed the soldier, when she hit his head with the water pitcher? She was scared in the dark alley and her mind felt splintered. If only there was someone with her! If only she could hunt down Honey Brown and they could go away together! But Honey had gone to Forks Falls and would not be back until tomorrow. Or if she could find the monkey and the monkey-man and join with them to run away! There was a scuttling noise, and she jerked with terror. A cat had leaped up on a garbage can, and in the darkness she could see its outline against the light at the end of the alley. She whispered: 'Charles!' and then 'Charlina.' But it was not her Persian cat, and when she stumbled towards the can it sprang away.

She could stand the black sour alley no longer and, carrying the suitcase towards the light at the end, she stood close to the sidewalk, but still inside the shadow of a wall. If there was only somebody to tell her what to do and where to go and how to get there! The fortune of Big Mama had turned out true – about the sort of trip and a departure and a return, and even the cotton bales, for the bus had passed a truck of them on the way back from Winter Hill. And there was the sum of money in her father's wallet, so that already she had lived up all the fortune Big Mama had foreseen. Should she go down to the house in Sugarville and say that she had used up the whole future, and what was she now to do?

Beyond the shadow of the alley the gloomy street was like a street that waited, with the winking neon Coca-Cola sign on the next corner, and a lady walking back and forth beneath a street light as though expecting someone. A car, a long closed car that maybe was a Packard, came slowly down the street, and the way it cruised close to the kerb reminded her of a gangster's car, so that she shrank back closer to the wall. Then, on the opposite sidewalk, two people passed, and a feeling like a sudden flame sprang up inside her, and for less than a second it seemed that her brother and the bride had come for her and were now *there*. But the feeling blew out instantly and she was just watching a stranger couple passing down the street. There was a hollow in her chest, but at the bottom of this emptiness a heavy weight pressed down and bruised her stomach, so that she felt sick. She told herself she ought to get busy and pick up her feet and go away. But she still stood there, her eyes closed, and her head against the warm brick wall.

When she left the alley, it was a long time after midnight and she had reached the point where any sudden idea seemed a good idea. She had seized on first one notion and then another. To hitch-hike to Forks Falls and track down Honey, or to wire Evelyn Owen to meet her in Atlanta, or even to go back to the house and get John Henry, so that at least there would be somebody with her and she would not have to go into the world alone. But there was some objection to each of these ideas.

Then, all at once, from the tangle of turning impossibilities, she thought of the soldier; and this time the thought was not a glancing one – it lingered, stuck, and did not go away. She wondered if she ought to go to the Blue Moon and find if she had killed the soldier, before she left the town for ever. The idea, once seized on, seemed to her good, and she started for Front Avenue. If she had not killed the soldier, then when she found him what could she say? How the next thought occurred to her she did not know, but suddenly it seemed she might as well ask the soldier to marry with her, and then the two of them could go away. Before he had gone crazy, he had been a little nice. And because it was a new and sudden idea, it also seemed reasonable. She remembered a part of the fortune she had forgotten, that she would marry a light-haired person with blue eyes, and the fact that the soldier had light red hair and blue eyes were like a proof that this was the right thing to do.

She hurried faster. The night before was like a time that had happened so long ago that the soldier was unravelled in her memory. But she recalled the silence in the hotel room; and all at once a fit in a front room, the silence, the nasty talk behind the garage – these separate recollections fell together in the darkness of her mind, as shafting searchlights meet in the night sky upon an aeroplane, so that in a flash there came in her an understanding. There was a feeling of cold surprise; she stopped a minute, then went on towards the Blue Moon. The stores were dark and closed, the pawnshop window locked with criss-crossed steel against night robbers, and the only lights were those from the open wooden stairs of buildings and the greenish splash of brightness from the Blue Moon. There was a sound of quarrelling voices from an upper storey, and the footsteps of two men, far down the street, walking away. She was no longer thinking of the soldier; the discovery of the moment before had scattered him from her mind. There was only knowing that she must find somebody, anybody, that she could join with to go away. For now she admitted she was too scared to go into the world alone.

She did not leave the town that night, for the Law caught her in the Blue Moon. Officer Wylie was there when she walked in, although she did not see him until she was settled at the window table with the suitcase on the floor beside her. The juke-box sounded a sleazy blues and the Portuguese owner stood with his eyes closed, playing up and down the wooden counter in time to the sad juke-box tune. There were only a few people in a corner booth and the blue light gave the place a look of being under-seas. She did not see the Law until he was standing beside the table, and when she looked up at him, her startled heart quivered a little and then stopped still.

'You're Royal Addams's daughter,' the Law said, and her head admitted with a nod. 'I'll phone in to headquarters to say you're found. Just stay right here.'

The Law went back to the telephone booth. He was calling the Black Maria to haul her off down to the jail, but she did not care. Very likely she had killed that soldier, and they had been following clues and hunting her all over town. Or the Law maybe had found out about the three-way knife she had stolen from the Sears and Roebuck store. It was not plain just what she was captured for, and the crimes of the long spring and summer merged together as one guilt which she had lost the power to understand. It was as though the things that she had done, the sins committed, had all been done by someone else – a stranger a long time ago. She sat very still, her legs wrapped tight around each other, and her hands clasped in her lap. The Law was a long time at the telephone, and, staring straight ahead of her, she watched two people leave a booth and, leaning close against each other, start to dance. A soldier banged the screen door and walked through the café, and only the distant stranger in her recognized him; when he had climbed up the stairs, she only thought slowly and with no feeling that a curly red head such as that one was like cement. Then her mind went back to thoughts of jail and cold peas and cold cornbread and iron-barred cells. The Law came back from the telephone and sat down across from her and said:

'How did you happen to come in here?'

The Law was big in his blue policeman's suit and, once arrested, it was a bad policy to lie or trifle. He had a heavy face, with a squatty forehead and unmatched ears – one ear was larger than the other one, and had a torn look. When he questioned her, he did not look into her face, but at some point just above her head.

'What am I doing in here?' she repeated. For all at once she had forgotten, and she told the truth when she said finally, 'I don't know.'

The voice of the Law seemed to come from a distance like a question asked through a long corridor. 'Where were you headed for?'

The world was now so far away that Frances could no longer think of it. She did not see the earth as in the old days, cracked and loose and turning a thousand miles an hour; the earth was enormous and still and flat. Between herself and all the places there was a space like an enormous canyon she could not hope to bridge or cross. The plans for the movies or the Marines were only child plans that would never work, and she was careful when she answered. She named the littlest, ugliest place she knew, for to run away there could not be considered so very wrong.

'Flowering Branch.'

'Your father phoned headquarters you had left a letter that you were running away. We located him at the bus station and he'll be here in a minute to take you home.'

It was her father who had sicked the Law on her, an she would not be carried to the jail. In a way she was sorry. It was better to be in a jail where you could bang the walls than in a jail you could not see. The world was too far away, and there was no way any more that she could be included. She was back to the fear of the summertime, the old feelings that the world was separate from herself – and the failed wedding had quickened the fear to terror. There had been a time, only yesterday, when she felt that every person that she saw was somehow connected with herself and there was between the two of them an instant recognition. Frances watched the Portuguese who still played a mock piano on the counter to the juke-box tune. He swayed as he played and his fingers skittered up and down the counter, so that a man at the far end protected his glass with his hand. When the tune was over, the Portuguese folded his arms upon his chest; Frances narrowed and tensed her eyes to will him to look at her. He had been the first person she had told the day before about the wedding, but as he gave an owner's look around the place, his glance passed by her in a casual way and there was in those eyes no feeling of connexion. She turned to the others in the room, and it was the same with all of them and they were strangers. In the blue light she felt queer as a person drowning. At last she was staring at the Law and finally he looked into her eyes. He looked at her with eyes as china as a doll's, and in them there was only the reflection of her own lost face.

The screen door slammed and the Law said: 'Here's your Daddy come to take you home.'

Frances was never once to speak about the wedding. Weathers had turned and it was in another season. There were the changes and Frances was now thirteen. She was in the kitchen with Berenice on the day before they moved, the last afternoon that Berenice would be with them; for when it had been decided that she and her father would share with Aunt Pet and Uncle Ustace a house out in the new suburb of town, Berenice had given quit notice and said that she might as well marry T.T. It was the end of an afternoon in late November, and in the east the sky was the colour of a winter geranium

Frances had come back to the kitchen, for the other rooms were hollow since the van had taken the furniture away. There were only two beds in the downstairs bedrooms and the kitchen furniture, and they were to be moved tomorrow. It was the first time in a long while that Frances had spent an afternoon back in the kitchen, alone with Berenice. It was not the same kitchen of the summer that now seemed so long ago. The pencil pictures had disappeared beneath a coat of calcimine, and new linoleum covered the splintery floor. Even the table had been moved, pushed back against the wall, since now there was nobody to take meals with Berenice.

The kitchen, done over and almost modern, had nothing that would bring to mind John Henry West. But nevertheless there were times when Frances felt his presence there, solemn and hovering and ghost-grey. And at those times there would come a hush – a hush quivered by voiceless words. A similar hush would come, also, when Honey was mentioned or brought to mind, for Honey was out on the road now with a sentence of eight years. Now the hush came that late November afternoon as Frances was making the sandwiches, cutting them into fancy shapes and taking great pains – for Mary Littlejohn was coming at five o'clock. Frances glanced at Berenice, who was sitting idle in a chair, wearing an old ravelled sweater, her limp arms hanging at her sides. In her lap there was the thin little pinched fox fur that Ludie had given her many years ago. The fur was sticky and the sharp little face foxwise and sad. The fire from the red stove brushed the room with flickers of light and changing shadows.

'I am just mad about Michelangelo,' she said.

Mary was coming at five o'clock to take dinner, spend the night, and ride in the van to the new house tomorrow. Mary collected pictures of great masters and pasted them in an art book. They read poets like Tennyson together; and Mary was going to be a great painter and Frances a great poet – or else the foremost authority on radar. Mr Littlejohn had been connected with a tractor company and before the war the Littlejohns had lived abroad. When Frances was sixteen and Mary eighteen, they were going around the world together. Frances placed the sandwiches on a plate, along with eight chocolates and some salted nuts; this was to be a midnight feast, to be eaten in the bed at twelve o'clock.

'I told you we're going to travel around the world together.'

'Mary Littlejohn,' said Berenice, in a tinged voice. 'Mary Littlejohn.'

Berenice could not appreciate Michel-angelo or poetry, let alone Mary Littlejohn. There had at first been words between them on the subject. Berenice had spoken of Mary as being lumpy and marshmallow-white, and Frances had defended fiercely. Mary had long braids that she could very nearly sit on, braids of a woven mixture of corn-yellow and brown, fastened at the ends with rubber bands and, on occasions, ribbons. She had brown eyes with yellow eyelashes, and her dimpled hands tapered at the fingers to little pink blobs of flesh, as Mary bit her nails. The Littlejohns were Catholics, and even on this point Berenice was all of a sudden narrow-minded, saying that Roman Catholics worshipped Graven Images and wanted the Pope to rule the world. But for Frances this difference was a final touch of strangeness, silent terror, that completed the wonder of her love.

'There's no use in our discussing a certain party. You could not possibly ever understand her. It's just not in you.' She had said that once before to Berenice, and from the sudden faded stillness in her eyes she knew that the words had hurt. And now she repeated them, angered because of the tinged way Berenice had said the name, but once the words were spoken she was sorry. 'Anyhow, I consider it the greatest honour of my existence that Mary has picked me out to be her one most intimate friend. Me! Of all people!'

'Have I ever said anything against her?' said Berenice. 'All I said was it makes me nervous to watch her just sitting there sucking them pigtails.'

'Braids!'

A flock of strong-winged arrowed geese flew over the yard, and Frances went to the window. There had been frost that morning, silvering the brown grass and the roofs of neighbours' houses, and even the thinned leaves of the rusty arbour. When she turned back to the kitchen, the hush was in the room again. Berenice sat hunched with her elbow on her knee, and her forehead resting in her hand, staring with one mottled eye at the coal scuttle.

The changes had come about at the same time, during the middle of October. Frances had met Mary at a raffle two weeks before. It was the time when countless white and yellow butterflies danced among the last fall flowers; the time, too, of the Fair. First, it was Honey. Made crazy one night by a marihuana cigarette, by something called smoke or snow, he broke into the drugstore of the white man who had been selling them to him, desperate for more. He was locked in the jail, awaiting trial, and Berenice rushed back and forth, canvassing money, seeing a lawyer, and trying to get admission to the jail. She came in on the third day, worn out, and with the red curdled glare already in the eye. A headache, she said she had, and John Henry West put his head down on the table and said he had a headache, also. But nobody paid any mind to him, thinking he copied Berenice. 'Run along,' she said, 'for I don't have the patience to fool with you.' Those were the last words spoken to him in the kitchen, and later Berenice recalled them as judgement on her from the Lord. John Henry had meningitis and after ten days he was dead. Until it was all over, Frances had never believed for a serious minute that he could die. It was the time of golden weather and Shasta daisies and the butterflies. The air was chilled, and day after day the sky was a clear green-blue, but filled with light, the colour of a shallow wave.

Frances was never allowed to visit John Henry, but Berenice helped the trained nurse every day. She would come in towards dark, and the things that she said in her cracked voice seemed to make John Henry West unreal. 'I don't see why he has to suffer so,' Berenice would say: and the word *suffer* was one she could not associate with John Henry, a word she shrank from as before an unknown hollow darkness of the heart.

It was the time of the Fair and a big banner arched the main street and for six days and nights the Fair went on down at the fairground. Frances went twice, both times with Mary, and they rode on nearly everything, but did not enter the Freak Pavilion, as Mrs Littlejohn said it was morbid to gaze at Freaks. Frances bought John Henry a walking stick and sent him the rug she had won at Lotto. But Berenice remarked that he was beyond all this, and the words were eerie and unreal. As the bright days followed one upon the other, the words of Berenice became so terrible that she would listen in a spell of horror, but a part of her could not believe. John Henry had been screaming for three days and his eyeballs were walled up in a corner, stuck and blind. He lay there finally with his head drawn back in a buckled way, and he had lost the strength to scream. He died the Tuesday after the Fair was gone, a golden morning of the most butterflies, the clearest sky.

Meanwhile Berenice had got a lawyer and had seen Honey at the jail. 'I don't know what I've done,' she kept saying. 'Honey in this fix and now John Henry.' Still, there was some part of Frances that did not even yet believe. But on the day he was to be taken to the family graveyard in Opelika, the same place where they had buried Uncle Charles, she saw the coffin, and then she knew. He came to her once or twice in nightmare dreams, like an escaped child dummy from the window of a department store, the wax legs moving stiffly only at joints, and the wax face wizened and faintly painted, coming towards her until terror snatched her awake. But the dreams came only once or twice, and the daytime was now filled with radar, school, and Mary Littlejohn. She remembered John Henry more as he used to be, and it was seldom now that she felt his presence – solemn, hovering, and ghost-grey. Only occasionally at twilight time or when the special hush would come into the room.

'I was by the store about school and Papa

had a letter from Jarvis. He is in Luxembourg,' said Frances. 'Luxembourg. Don't you think that's a lovely name?'

Berenice roused herself. 'Well, Baby – it brings to my mind soapy water. But it's a kind of pretty name.'

'There is a basement in the new house. And a laundry room.' She added, after a minute. 'We will most likely pass through Luxembourg when we go around the world together.'

Frances turned back to the window. It was almost five o'clock and the geranium glow had faded from the sky. The last pale colours were crushed and cold on the horizon. Dark, when it came, would come on quickly, as it does in wintertime. 'I am simply mad about–' But the sentence was left unfinished for the hush was shattered when, with an instant shock of happiness, she heard the ringing of the bell.

The publishers hope that this book has given you enjoyable reading. Large Print Books are especially designed to be as easy to see and hold as possible. If you wish a complete list of our books please ask at your local library or write directly to:

Dales Large Print Books
Magna House, Long Preston,
Skipton, North Yorkshire.
BD23 4ND

This Large Print Book, for people
who cannot read normal print,
is published under the auspices of

THE ULVERSCROFT FOUNDATION

... we hope you have enjoyed this book.
Please think for a moment about those
who have worse eyesight than you ...
and are unable to even read or enjoy
Large Print without great difficulty.

You can help them by sending a
donation, large or small, to:

**The Ulverscroft Foundation,
1, The Green, Bradgate Road,
Anstey, Leicestershire, LE7 7FU,
England.**
or request a copy of our brochure for
more details.

The Foundation will use all donations
to assist those people who are visually
impaired and need special attention
with medical research, diagnosis
and treatment.

Thank you very much for your help.